SCIENTIFIC DECEPTION

AN OVERVIEW AND GUIDE TO THE
LITERATURE OF MISCONDUCT AND
FRAUD IN SCIENTIFIC RESEARCH

By LESLEY GRAYSON

THE BRITISH LIBRARY

Scientific Deception: an overview and guide to the literature of misconduct and fraud in scientific research
ISBN 0-7123-0831-8

Published by:

The British Library
Science Reference and Information Service
25 Southampton Buildings
London WC2A 1AW

© 1995 The British Library Board

British Library Cataloguing-in-Publication Data
A catalogue record for this book is available from the British Library

For further information on publications produced by The British Library Science
Reference and Information Service (SRIS) contact Paul Wilson, SRIS,
25 Southampton Buildings, London WC2A 1AW. Tel: 0171-412 7472.

Desktop publishing by Concerto, Leighton Buzzard, Bedfordshire. Tel: 01525 378757.

Printed by Hobbs the Printers Ltd, Totton, Hampshire SO40 3YS.

SCIENTIFIC DECEPTION

CONTENTS

PREFACE

The main title of this review avoids the terms misconduct or fraud, but the literature of scientific deception covering these latter words is extensive and wide ranging. The author has included material from a wide range of disciplines and indeed countries, and whilst many of the cases discussed emanate from the medical research world in the United States, it is clear that scientific deception in its widest sense is a much greater problem than many in the international scientific establishment would have us believe.

The review is necessarily selective, but it focuses on reality rather than the theory of scientific deception and on the policy implications which may arise. As such, it is a valuable introduction to some of the complex issues associated with scientific deception and to the responses which the research community might well consider appropriate.

The review is one of a number of titles published by the British Library Science Reference and Information Service in recent years in its science policy series. These highlight relevant and occasionally contentious issues in science and technology policy using the vast information resources of the Library to identify the most important documents on particular topics. Other recent titles in the series include *Science Parks: an experiment in high technology transfer* (1993), and *Inward Investment* (in preparation 1995). The review is fully indexed and most of the references cited are available from the British Library Document Supply Centre at Boston Spa in Yorkshire or the British Library science reference collections in the Science Reference and Information Service Reading Rooms at either Kean Street or 25 Southampton Buildings in central London.

Alan Gomersall
Director
British Library Science Reference and Information Service
September 1995

ABOUT THE AUTHOR

Lesley Grayson is a freelance writer and editor specialising in literature-based guides on topics of interest for policy makers, researchers and practitioners. She is editor of The British Library journal *Science, Technology and Innovation*; editor of the public policy review series *Inlogov Informs* published by the University of Birmingham Institute of Local Government Studies; and author of a range of information guides, principally on environmental and social policy issues.

INTRODUCTION

'The right to search for truth implies also a duty: one must not conceal any part of what one has recognized to be true.' (A Einstein)

The belief that scientific investigation is a quest for objective truth remains embedded in the popular consciousness. In the public mind, the scientist has a unique mission to uncover and explain reality for the benefit of society at large through the development of hypotheses, experimentation and verification. This disinterested pursuit of truth does not rule out normal human fallibility: mistakes can happen, scientists can be deluded, but the nature of scientific method (especially the requirement for publication and verification) ensures that truth will out in the end.

The notion that scientists might deliberately violate ethical norms of conduct for personal gain or gratification is deeply shocking to many people despite the fact that such violations in other areas of life may be viewed much more tolerantly. By breaching the responsibility to report accurately and faithfully the results of experimental investigations, such behaviour undermines the entire nature of the scientific enterprise which is believed to operate on a different plane from other kinds of human activity. The belief in the essential objectivity of scientific knowledge, and in its supposed power to cure all manner of ills and foster human progress, confers a special status on scientists and sets them apart from the normal run of humankind. In the past this often meant an uncritical acceptance, even reverence, for science and scientists.

Ambiguous science

Today things are very different. Declining respect for science is an inevitable result of greater public education and of the increasing intervention of science into the everyday concerns of ordinary people. One has only to open a newspaper to find evidence of the fallibility or ambiguity of 'objective' scientific knowledge. Opposing camps in debates on issues such as acid rain, food safety, nuclear waste disposal, lead pollution and, most recently, the disposal of spent oil platforms are seen to present sometimes diametrically opposed conclusions based on identical data. The reality of scientific investigation is being exposed to the public gaze as never before - not as the clinical uncovering of some unequivocal truth, but as a process deeply influenced by a complex series of personal choices and subjective interpretations prompted by both internal and external factors.

It is doubtful whether the bulk of ordinary people recognise the implications of what they read in their newspapers - that the scientific endeavour is, in many ways, no different from any other human activity, and that scientific 'truth' is almost always qualified in some way. The sight of warring scientists each presenting data to support the standpoint of their own camps is more likely to lead to a cynical assumption that such individuals have sold out to special interests. However, belief in the essential objectivity of scientific knowledge - in the existence of 'truth' despite the efforts of special interest groups to subvert it to their own ends - may well still persist. The apparent conflict between the observed behaviour of some scientists and the supposed nature of the endeavour in which they are engaged has undoubtedly played an important role in forming late twentieth century attitudes towards scientists.

Certainly there are no signs of a more forgiving attitude towards scientific fraud which continues to attract a degree of public attention probably out of all proportion to its incidence in the scientific community. Perhaps this is not surprising given the fact that many of the most notorious recent cases involve the biomedical sciences which are, inevitably, of direct personal relevance to many people: the forging of archaeological artefacts or fossils may, for example, be of passing interest to the layman, but the falsifying of data in breast cancer or AIDS research is quite another matter.

Deception and the scientific process

The main title of this literature review has deliberately avoided the words misconduct or fraud in favour of the term deception which can cover a wide range of behaviours, both conscious and unconscious. Among the references which follow there are many case studies of outright fraud, often from the United States, but there is a sense in which concentration on these more blatant examples of scientific misconduct can obscure deeper and more worrying issues. In particular, it allows the scientific establishment to take comfort in the belief that deception is a rare, though serious, problem often prompted by individual psychological or psychiatric factors. Moreover, it may claim that both deception and honest errors will inevitably be revealed by the self-correcting mechanisms which are characteristic of the scientific process.

This view accepts that external factors may have a part to play in deception – for example, the pressure to publish as a means of gaining promotion or new research grants – but it does not explicitly recognise that the nature of the scientific process itself may be conducive of such behaviour on a much wider level. Because scientific investigation involves a multiplicity of choices, and is open to contamination at a variety of levels (there is no such thing as a 'pure' research environment), there are many points at which conscious or unconscious bias and/or deception can creep in. This might be based on the scientist's personal passion for a particular theory or, conversely, an unwillingness to challenge orthodoxy. It may, in some cases, be based on political leanings, or on varying degrees of pressure from a sponsor to produce the 'right' result at the right time.

According to one analyst, Beth Savan, 'the pursuit of desired scientific results, through the choice of experimental methods, analytical techniques, interpretations, or reporting formats is probably common'. In Savan's view, scientists are just as prone as the rest of us to shape knowledge in line with preconceived views or external pressures (although they may often have higher ethical standards), and the inherent ambiguity of the research process allows them ample opportunity to do so. This should not be taken as a criticism of scientists, merely an acceptance that they are human.

The adverse effects of error, bias and deception are, in the conventional view, eliminated by the self-correcting mechanisms of science. These include the operation of peer review in the selection of research projects for funding and in the choice of scientific papers for publication, and the process of experimental replication and verification. However, it is clear that these mechanisms do not always work very effectively. Peer review has come under attack for inherent conservatism, prejudice and sloppiness and, when deception is revealed, it is often difficult to ensure that fraudulent data and analysis are formally retracted. Equally, belief in the power of experimental replication may be misplaced. The exact replication of someone else's work is not a popular area of activity for scientists, and is relatively rare except in cases where the original findings are particularly momentous or anomalous. Thus the effects of deception or error may remain undetected for many years, while the producers of the original fraudulent data can always attribute discrepancies to, for example, slight differences in experimental procedures.

Responses to deception

Regulatory and other measures to control the rare cases of deliberate fraud are certainly needed given the damage which they may cause - not only to the individuals involved but to unwitting collaborators, the rest of the research community which uses fraudulent data in good faith, funding bodies (including government) whose resources have been misappropriated, and ordinary members of the public. The last may suffer not only as taxpayers but as recipients of services corrupted in some way by scientific deception. In the biomedical field, which attracts most public attention, the dangers may be obvious, but there are other examples including the influence on the English education system of the IQ research of Sir Cyril Burt, although recent comment suggests that the malpractice allegations against Burt may have been malicious. (In the general context of policy making, as opposed to clinical practice, bias and deception in the social sciences could be of much more significance than in the natural sciences - and even harder to detect.)

Attempts to identify exactly what constitutes deliberate scientific deception, to detect and prevent it, and to institute appropriate disciplinary procedures have occupied the minds of many in the scientific community, especially in the United States. There have, for example, been impassioned debates about the relative merits of self-regulation as against intervention by governmental or judicial bodies which have yet to be resolved. However, it could be argued that these initiatives focus on only a tiny part of the problem, what might be termed the criminal end of the deception spectrum. The allegedly much more pervasive, if less dramatic, bias and deception (conscious and unconscious) which occurs as a result of the normal operation of the scientific process under modern conditions may be far more significant in terms of the public good. If looked at in these terms, the impact of a single blatantly fraudulent scientist, whose activities will almost certainly come to light eventually, may be far less serious than the cumulative effects of everyday, small scale and largely invisible deceptions prompted by external pressures and vested interests.

This view of the deception problem would, of course, encompass the kind of legalistic approaches designed for the abnormal or criminal end of science. However, policy responses would be much broader in scope, recognising the fact that science, like other human activities, is influenced by vested interests and that the public good is best served by making these relationships as transparent as possible. It would address issues such as deficiencies in the self-correcting mechanisms of science including the operation of peer review and scientific publishing, the implications of the hierarchical organisation of research institutions, the potential for conflicts of interest between researchers and their sources of funding, the ethical training and supervision of young scientists - all matters relating to the normal practice of science.

Many initiatives of this kind are already underway, again particularly in the United States, and some may have quite radical implications for the traditional practice of science if carried to their logical conclusions. Scientists might, for example, be required to disclose all corporate, commercial, governmental and advocacy group affiliations when applying for research funding or acting as peer reviewers. Equally, an acceptance that vested interests have an inescapable influence on science may lead to demands for a much more pluralistic system in which innovative and minority viewpoints on a given scientific issue are actively courted alongside the more conventional. The public and their representatives might find it no easier to decide between the competing claims of different camps, but at least they would have a broader base of information on which to make choices. Such an approach could cause a revolution in the normally conservative practice of peer review, and in the hierarchical management of research laboratories.

A greater understanding of the complex reality of the scientific process and the many pressures exerted on scientists may also lead to a more explicit focus on the implications for scientific deception of government science policies. If science is embedded in, and influenced by, a complex web of personal and organisational vested interests, it is reasonable to suppose that such policies will play an important role in determining how scientists work. It has, for example, been plausibly argued that UK government insistence on quantitative measures of research excellence has intensified the already inexorable pressure to publish, a factor long recognised as one of those contributing to scientific deception. Equally, government pressure on universities to derive an increasing proportion of their research income from the private sector may increase the dangers involved in closer academic-industry relations. None of this is to say that deception is an inevitable result of such policy trends, merely that it would be prudent to recognise the pressures which they may put on the researcher.

The literature of scientific deception

The literature of scientific deception, broadly defined, is extensive and wide ranging. It includes material from the sociology, psychology, philosophy and history of science as well as descriptive and analytical studies of particular cases, studies of the scientific publishing and peer review systems, ethical guidance documents for researchers and scientific institutions, and policy responses. There is a great deal of 'newsy' material on cases and policy developments in American journals such as *Science, Science and Government Report, Scientist, Chemical and Engineering News,* the *New England Journal of Medicine, IEEE Engineering in Medicine and Biology* and the *Journal of the American Medical Association.* In Britain, news coverage is provided by *Nature,* the *Lancet,* the *British Medical Journal* and *New Scientist.*

Those wishing to maintain a watching brief on developments would be well advised to concentrate on these sources. However, material can also be identified via bibliographic databases in the sciences. Among the most useful is Bioethicsline, a database produced by the Kennedy Institute of Ethics at Georgetown University under contract to the US National Library of Medicine. This includes articles from approximately 100 journal titles as well as books, reports, court cases, bills and audiovisual media. It covers the period from 1973 onwards and is available as a CD-ROM, updated every four months, at the Wellcome Centre for Medical Science Information Service, 183 Euston Road, London NW1 2BE or online via Blaise-Link from The British Library, Health Care Information Service, 25 Southampton Buildings, London WC2A 1AW.

Other relevant databases such as BIOSIS and SciSearch can be accessed through the on-line search service at the British Library's Science Reference and Information Service (25 Southampton Buildings, London WC2A 1AW) and much of the journal literature in this review can be found in the SRIS reading rooms at Southampton Buildings and at 9 Kean Street, London WC2B 4AT where life sciences material is housed. Other material is available (via the reader's own library) from the Library's Document Supply Centre, Boston Spa, Wetherby, West Yorkshire LS23 7BQ.

Much of the literature is American, or relates to American experience, because it is here that professional and policy concerns about scientific deception have been explored most fully. Although US policy responses at the government level may be inappropriate for other countries, American studies of the nature, causes and potential remedies for deception are often relevant given the international character of scientific investigation, and the existence of some common science policy trends among the advanced nations.

A selective view

This review is necessarily selective. For example, it makes no attempt to cover in detail the more arcane studies of the nature of scientific truth, scientific method or scientific deviance, many of which are viewed with scepticism by the scientific community. Nor does it look in detail at specific cases of deception although many are discussed at length in the books, journal articles and reports listed in the review. Many of these have extensive bibliographies which give access to the wider literature for those interested in the history and academic analysis of the deception problem. It tries to focus on the reality rather than the theory of the scientific endeavour, and on the policy implications which may arise, in so far as these are reflected in the published literature.

The material is presented in three chapters dealing with the scientific process; the pressures on scientists; and responses and policy implications. In each case, a short analytical review of the issues precedes the bibliographical listings which are given in chronological order of publication to allow readers to trace the development of thinking, policy or practice. Where specific documents are referred to in the text, their reference numbers are given, but readers should be aware that it is impossible to do full justice to the complexity of the literature in a review of this length. Although the text provides a brief introduction to some of the issues, there is a great deal more information in the listings which are annotated wherever possible.

In deference to the importance of transparency, it should be noted that the objectivity of the review is compromised by a number of factors: the limitations of literature searching on bibliographic databases, particularly in a social science area such as this; the subjective influences on the selection process exercised by the compiler's personal prejudices and interests; and resource constraints both of time and money. That said, the aim is to provide at least an introduction to some of the complex issues associated with scientific deception and to the responses which might be appropriate.

The UK scene

Those looking for specifically UK material on scientific deception will be largely disappointed. Although the Royal College of Physicians and the Association of the British Pharmaceutical Industry have produced reports and guidance on the issues, there is relatively little documented evidence of deception in the UK. Nor do the research councils, individual universities or government appear to have a published view. However, there is increasing pressure from some quarters, principally the *British Medical Journal* and the *Lancet*, for concerted action including the establishment of an independent investigatory body.

The recent case of Dr Malcolm Pearce, a senior consultant at St George's Hospital in London, may prove to be a turning point in British attitudes to the problem of scientific deception. The speed and vigour with which his alleged falsification of data on a treatment for ectopic pregnancy was investigated and disciplined are unique, and influential elements in the biomedical research community are now quite clear about the dangers such behaviour poses. Not only is it damaging to science and to the reputations of those unwittingly caught up in fraudulent activities, it threatens public confidence in the integrity of science. 'Science', according to the registrar of the Royal College of Physicians, 'is a delicate plant which can't afford to have its reputation damaged'. In the aftermath of the Pearce case, the Royal College took a policy decision to begin exploring the issues involved in setting up some form of independent investigatory body.

Conclusion

However, in the UK as in the USA where the whole issue of deception is discussed much more openly, much of the scientific community still tends to respond with shock and disbelief to evidence of misconduct. The overwhelming priority is to claim that the problem is rare and to attribute it to individual mental aberration. Those who unmask the deception - the whistleblowers - often suffer more than the perpetrators, even in the United States where they are offered a degree of formal protection. In this respect the scientific community is little different from other professional groups who find it difficult to accept evidence of the violation of ethical norms and close ranks in support of accused members.

It is, perhaps, time to recognise openly that a very few scientists do deliberately set out to deceive on the grand scale, and develop measures to detect and deal with the problem. Equally, it may be necessary to admit publicly that the scientific process itself is riddled with opportunities for bias of various kinds which may shade into deception, and certainly make a nonsense of the 'objectivity' of scientific knowledge. The scientific community can rightly be proud of the high ethical principles followed by most of its members, but cannot deny that they are as influenced by personal ambition, professional enthusiasms, political leanings and corporate pressures as everyone else. Finally, it is incumbent on government to be aware of the potential impact of its policies on the scientific process, particularly those designed to increase research productivity and accountability, link research more closely with wealth creation objectives, or push academic researchers into greater dependence on corporate sources of funding.

Acknowledgements

Particular thanks are due to the following:

Paula Owen of the British Library's Science Reference and Information Service (SRIS) on-line search service, and Dr Paul Baxter and Dr Richard Wakeford of SRIS for comments and suggestions on the text.

Sue Spedding and her staff at the British Library Document Supply Centre Reading Room in Boston Spa for supplying many journal articles, books and reports.

The American Association for the Advancement of Science; Harvard University Faculty of Medicine; Sigma Xi (The Scientific Research Society); the Danish Medical Research Council; and the Association of the British Pharmaceutical Industry for supplying copies of their own publications on scientific deception.

Jean Moran, medical writer and researcher, for her help on the European Commission's standards of good clinical practice in trials of medicinal products.

Lesley Grayson
September 1995

1. THE SCIENTIFIC PROCESS

The traditional view of the scientific endeavour is a markedly high minded one, and still exercises a considerable influence over public perceptions. Indeed, the noticeable decline in respect for scientists in recent decades may in one sense be attributed to a belief that they have betrayed the principles of this endeavour for reasons of politics or personal gain. Many people would, no doubt, still subscribe to the view of sociologist Robert K Merton who argued that science is principally the disinterested pursuit of truth and only secondarily a means of earning a living. In his classic analysis of *The normative structure of science* (Ref. 3), he describes the scientific endeavour as governed by a series of cognitive or technical norms dealing with issues such as experimental design and the analysis of evidence, and a series of moral or social norms. The latter have been renamed, and added to, in subsequent years but remain central to the conventional view of science.

Universalism – a norm which emphasises the importance of objective, impersonal criteria in scientific advance. Among other things it includes a disavowal of appeals to a scientist's race, nationality, class and personal characteristics.

Communality – the substantive findings of science are the product of social collaboration and are assigned to the community as a common heritage. Intellectual property protection may produce tensions, but does not invalidate the concept of communality.

Disinterestedness – scientists should be motivated by a search for the truth, not biased towards pet hypotheses or concerned with the active pursuit of personal advancement.

Organised scepticism – scientific claims must be subjected to 'detached scrutiny' through a process of public verification.

Such norms are commonly translated into ethical principles which may, as noted in Chapter 3, form the basis of published guidance for scientists. Examples include the *Principles of biomedical ethics* adopted by the President's Commission for the Study of Ethical Problems in Medicine and Biomedical and Behavioral Research in the United States (Ref. 28). They include principles such as autonomy (respect for individual self-determination); nonmaleficence (doing no harm, preventing harm and removing harmful conditions); and justice (giving each person what he or she is deserved or owed).

Thus, in the conventional view, scientific investigation is seen as the rational pursuit of objective truth which can be uncovered or explained through the development and testing of hypotheses using proven experimental techniques. Scientists are assumed to hold a set of moral values including an overriding commitment to truth in the face of pressures which might be exerted by financial inducements, the desire for professional advancement and other factors. Such a view does not rule out honest human error or self-deception, but science as a whole proceeds in the direction of truth because it is based on openness and the requirement for publication and verification of all experimental results. Deliberate deception is entirely attributable to individual personality defects, an isolated and extremely rare anomaly which will inevitably be brought to light by these self-correcting mechanisms.

Out of the ivory tower

This view of science held sway among the philosophers, sociologists and historians of science for many years, and is probably still in line with public opinion today. It also underpins the public utterances of many in the scientific establishment on the issue of deception. However, the 1960s saw the beginning of a change in attitudes with the publication of Thomas Kuhn's book, *The structure of scientific revolutions,* in 1962 (Ref. 2). This argued that scientific knowledge is not always the result of the rational, objective pursuit of truth by unbiased researchers.

Setting aside the philosophical arguments about whether objective truth exists at all, or practical doubts about how far scientific reporting is an accurate reflection of the reality of the research process (Ref. 10), the history of science shows that scientists tend to accumulate and shape knowledge in line with conventional wisdom to produce what Kuhn called 'normal science'. Only when the discrepancies between normal science and observed reality become overwhelming does science move forward, typically in a revolutionary way which can often consign earlier theories to the scientific dustbin even when they have value. Obvious examples include the watersheds between pre- and post-Copernican, pre- and post-Darwinian, and pre- and post-Einsteinian thinking.

Kuhn's views were extended in subsequent years by colleagues such as Harriet Zuckerman (Ref. 5) and challenged by other philosophers and sociologists of science. Paul Feyerabend, for example, in his influential book *Against method* (Ref. 4) argued that science was an essentially anarchistic enterprise in which knowledge may indeed expand on the basis of experimentation and replication, but can equally well advance as a result of luck or chance, and against all apparent reason – 'there is no idea, however ancient and absurd, that is not capable of improving our knowledge'. However extreme this thesis, and however much practising scientists may reject the theorising of philosophers and sociologists, the work of Kuhn, Feyerabend and others has been crucial in bringing science and scientists down from their ivory tower and into the real world: in the words of Karl Popper all human knowledge is human including science (Ref. 1).

Scientists may still be committed to uncovering external facts (the truth) but they do so on the basis of hypothesis and experimentation, both of which are deeply influenced by past knowledge and conventional wisdom as are all areas of human intellectual activity. Thus in a period of Kuhnian normal science, which may last decades or centuries, the scientific community will tend to exclude alternative or heretical explanations of a phenomenon. In the title of a recent book, such explanations become 'forbidden science' until the evidence in their favour becomes overwhelming (Ref. 46).

There is clearly ample scope for self-deception within science, maintained and reinforced by the inherent conservatism of intellectual progress and also by the occasional inexplicable credulity of the scientific profession (Ref. 21). The cold fusion saga is sometimes cited as an instance of the temporary mass suspension of critical faculties by otherwise sceptical scientists (Ref. 87, Ch. 2), and the strange polywater story of a decade or so before is another. Although initially reluctant to accept a Russian scientist's claim that he had discovered a new, denser form of water, the western scientific community invested enormous amounts of effort in trying to replicate his findings. One

US scientist described polywater as 'the most dangerous substance on earth' because the smallest drop might trigger the conversion of the world's water resources into a biologically useless form. Eventually the strange properties of polywater were attributed to simple laboratory contamination, to the embarrassment of hundreds of scientists and journal peer reviewers.

If scientific inquiry is subject to the foibles of human nature, there is also the possibility of deliberate deception in the pursuit of material gain, power or professional status. At the same time, the nature of scientific investigation offers numerous opportunities for misconduct. The process of developing a credible hypothesis and testing it is rarely as straightforward as the layman believes – there are always choices to made between alternative hypotheses, experimental techniques and methods of interpreting and presenting data; research environments are rarely completely pure; and instrumentation can be faulty. There are an almost infinite number of variables which can introduce bias, divert the honest scientist away from the truth, or offer the deceiver the opportunities he or she seeks. Sometimes the line between enthusiasm for a particular line of inquiry and deliberate corruption can be difficult to draw (Ref. 45).

A self-correcting system?

These problems are supposed to be resolved by the self-correcting mechanisms of science, principally peer review and the verification of experimental results. However, neither of these processes stand outside science and are just as prone to human frailty and the inherent ambiguities of scientific method as is original research. Peer review operates at both ends of the scientific process: in the evaluation of research proposals for funding purposes, and of research manuscripts for publication. The latter, in particular, has been widely criticised for conservatism, professional prejudice and sloppy standards, with several notorious cases of fraud escaping the notice of peer reviewers altogether. Moreover, as discussed more fully in the next chapter, journal peer review is under enormous stress because of the explosion in scientific publishing.

The second check on bias, deception and error is the replication of experiments. However, a fraudulent researcher can quite easily present fabricated data which represent a verifiable relationship (indeed, there would be little point in not doing so). Moreover, the exact replication of experiments is relatively rare except in cases where the results of the original research are particularly momentous or anomalous. Repeating someone else's work is, unsurprisingly, not a popular area of activity for most scientists, while financial cutbacks mean that many important studies are not repeated. Where they are, the lack of direct replication means that it can be almost impossible to identify the source of discrepancies between the results and those of the original research. In the event of a fraudulent scientist facing a challenge, it may be a relatively simple matter to attribute differences in findings to procedural variations. However, these problems may be particularly evident in the biomedical sciences and replication does apparently work effectively in some areas, for example theoretical physics (Ref. 16).

The Mertonian notion of science as a self-correcting system, though central to the scientific community's defence against the intervention of external monitoring and regulation, is now increasingly accepted as deficient. Indeed, regardless of the particular inadequacies of current peer review and replication systems, it is difficult to see how self-correction can possibly work effectively in a world in which the scientific endeavour has expanded so hugely and become so fragmented and specialised. Increasingly, scientists no longer have the time, resources, skills or knowledge to assess rigorously the work of colleagues, even those working in the same broad disciplinary area. Reliance on their honesty and professional capabilities may well seem the only practical way in which science can proceed.

The nature of deception

Much energy has been expended in trying to define what consitutes scientific deception, fraud or misconduct in a legalistic attempt to distinguish unacceptable from acceptable behaviour. Some kinds of behaviour – falsification of data, for example – clearly fall into the category of fraud and are almost universally condemned. However, there is a much wider range of less blatantly offensive practices which can be seen as deriving from the normal conduct of science in the modern world but may be equally damaging to science and the public good. Although it is obviously necessary to develop methods of detecting, preventing and punishing gross deception, it may be just as important to address these other practices and the environmental conditions which produce them. In this context, it may be necessary to refocus attention on the process of fraud, rather than the specific cases or behaviours which occupy most analysts (Ref. 44).

Beth Savan, in her book *Science under siege* (Ref. 121, Ch. 2) includes the following list of such behaviours, in descending order of seriousness:

'Invention of entire experiments, complete with fictitious results.

Invention of data. [And, one might add, fabrication of research materials or artefacts.]

Alteration of data.

Suppression of inconvenient data, either by omitting specific data points from a graph or report, or by failing to report an entire experiment.

Suppression of unwelcome projects, hypotheses, or findings by unwarranted rejection of manuscripts or grant applications.

Designing an experiment so that its results are inevitable and do not test any hypothesis.

Adoption of invalid or dubious assumptions that bias experimental results or interpretation; failure to retract publications of work that relied on assumptions now known to be invalid or dubious.

Analysing experimental results so that they appear to point in a predetermined direction.

Interpreting experimental results in a way that supports a particular theory, without exploring alternate interpretations.

Appropriation of research data produced by others for personal gain.

Presentation of others' data, analysis, or ideas without credit.

Systematic discrimination against particular individuals and institutions, and favouritism of others.

Republication of findings for personal gain without reference to their previous publication.'

Savan's list is not comprehensive and many other unethical behaviours of varying degrees of seriousness have been identified by other authors. These include the publication of multiple versions of the same research paper; unjustifiable authorship whereby individuals are named as authors when they have had little or nothing to do with the research; deliberate bias or delay in reviewing a research publication; the deliberate withholding of information in order to protect intellectual property; and stealing data or ideas from research proposals or papers under review. Malicious allegations of misconduct designed to sabotage the work of a competitor also fall within the broad definition of deceptive practices which may be detrimental to science and the public good to one degree or another (Ref. 47).

The problem of definition

However, merely listing unethical behaviours is of little practical value unless one can demonstrate which laws, rules or norms have been violated. The definition of what constitutes scientific deception in relation to these external criteria is seen as an essential precursor to the development of institutional responses to the problem, and has so far proved to be a major stumbling block which existing legislation seems powerless to overcome. While the laws of fraud, defamation, misrepresentation and copyright may offer some guidance at the more obviously 'criminal' end of the deception spectrum, there are major difficulties in applying them to cases of suspected scientific misconduct. Establishing intent to deceive is only one of these.

Moreover, many of the behaviours listed by Savan and others violate no laws at all, nor are they necessarily recognised as unethical by the scientific community. Even some of the grosser variants may be excused on the grounds of other overriding factors. For example, the potential conflict between a patient's best interests and the principles of scientific method is a persistent ethical dilemma in biomedical research. How is society to judge a doctor who deliberately falsifies data in order to increase a terminally ill patient's chances of being included in the trials of a new drug which may be that patient's only chance of survival (Ref. 23)?

Nor are the 'crimes' of plagiarism and theft of ideas always as clear cut as the lay observer might think. Although originality is seen as a key characteristic of good research, intellectual progress inevitably (and rightly) carries a large amount of baggage from the past. It is not always possible to distinguish between outright theft and the normal process of absorbing the ideas of one's intellectual peers or predecessors, nor is the attribution of discovery to particular individuals necessarily easy, especially in modern science where collaborative teamwork is increasingly the norm. Moreover, many undergraduate scientists may have only the haziest idea of what plagiarism means after years of school education in which the paraphrasing of work from secondary sources is not only acceptable but actively encouraged, while the techniques of proper referencing are virtually ignored. Without explicit instruction on the issues at an early stage in their university education, it is little wonder that some scientists find it difficult to accept that plagiarism is a cardinal sin.

Lower down the scale of seriousness there is even less agreement on the definition of deception (Ref. 41). Multiple publication of the same research paper or the inclusion of 'honorary' authors may, for example, be seen as essential (if regrettable) tactics in the cut-throat competition for research funding. Indeed, the author listings of some scientific papers now resemble American film credits in their length and comprehensive coverage. There has been a rapid increase in the number of life sciences papers with more than 100 authors, while a recent paper from the Fermi National Accelerator Laboratory announcing the discovery of the top quark listed nearly 400.

These trends are partly attributable to the power exercised by publications ratings and, while they may sometimes represent a kind of deception, many scientists would argue that they are an inescapable part of the modern scientific world and cannot, therefore, be described as morally reprehensible. Similar arguments might be advanced in explanation of the under-reporting of research evidence which casts doubt on a favoured hypothesis, or fails to provide a firm conclusion. There is enormous pressure on scientists to publish positive results, and this kind of fudging of evidence may be much more widespread than deliberate falsification (Ref. 30).

Scientific stonewalling

The difficulties involved in developing unambiguous definitions of what constitutes scientific deception, misconduct or fraud have occupied scientists and policy makers (mainly in America) in many hours of discussion, and have bedevilled the process of developing effective policy responses. The lack of agreed definitions means that it is impossible to provide objective data of how much deception there is. At the same time, standards of acceptable behaviour change in response to new conditions and make it difficult to judge whether the incidence of deception has changed over time. As a result, there is little 'hard' evidence beyond the rare and well-publicised incidents of gross fraud – only the anonymous evidence provided by scientists responding to opinion surveys. This often suggests a much higher incidence of deception than conventional wisdom allows, but its anecdotal nature has allowed elements in the scientific establishment to reject such evidence as unsubstantiated opinion and not worthy of consideration (Ref. 38).

Thus the definitional problem has proved a major force in support of the traditional view of deception as a rare phenomenon, attributable largely to the aberrant psychology of individuals, and one which the scientific community is well able to handle on its own in the time-honoured informal way. It has also allowed scientists to play down the impact on researchers of external pressures deriving from the ways in which science is organised, managed and funded, and to blame increased public concern about deception on an irresponsible press. However, these traditional defences are becoming increasingly untenable in a world in which the public funds a significant proportion of research, either through taxation or contributions to charity, and in which reverence and respect for the professions are breaking down in the face of greater public education, media attention, and (in the UK at least) assault from the political right wing. The ethos of science, with its emphasis on internalised standards, peer control and professional autonomy is seen to be at odds with the ethos of liberal democracy based on public scrutiny, control and accountability. In the modern world science is simply too important to be left to scientists (Ref. 8).

To some commentators the innate conservatism and complacency of the scientific community are so powerful that the public will never really appreciate what goes on behind the laboratory door without the intervention of some kind of independent force to investigate and prosecute suspected deception, and protect those who report it. John Postgate, emeritus professor of microbiology at the University of Sussex, might stand as a modern example of the traditional school of thinking: 'Science imposes a stern, austere morality upon its adherents, one which pervades their lives and outlooks...You advance neither knowledge nor your own reputation if you are guilty of deception, including self-deception; nor if you disregard unwelcome or inconsistent evidence; nor if you conceal rather than share data. Why? Because deception, plagiarism and falsification of evidence will be found out, usually very soon. Self-deception engenders contempt. Concealment, such as failure to publish, is self-defeating through loss of scientific credit. But, above all, such behaviour will delay scientific progress' (Ref. 49).

Postgate is convinced that 'the stern morality of science' makes it an infinitely better basis for the ordering of human society than religion, and that 'cheats, frauds and inadequates are remarkably rare among the scientific community, because all know that in the end such transgressions are pointless'. However, at least some of his fellow scientists may wonder whether Postgate is living in the real world with real people. An anonymous junior researcher contributing to a recent BBC *Horizon* programme on scientific deception puts the more cynical (or realistic) view: 'The public image of research scientists is that they are people with lofty ideals, toiling away selflessly for the good of mankind. I'm afraid the reality is that it's often a very sordid affair' (Ref 48).

(1)
CONJECTURE and refutations: the growth of scientific knowledge
Popper, K
Harper Torchbooks: New York, 1965. 417pp
A detailed analysis of the process of scientific advance as the constant interplay between imagination, intuition and hypothesis formation on the one hand, and the rigorous testing of hypotheses on the other. For a simpler exposition of these ideas
See also: Induction and intuition in scientific thought, by P B Medawar (American Philosophical Society: Philadephia, 1969. 62pp)

(2)
THE STRUCTURE of scientific revolutions: 2nd edition enlarged
Kuhn, T S
University of Chicago Press, 1970. 210pp (International Encyclopaedia of Unified Science, Vol. 2, No. 2)
Originally published in 1962. An influential work on the nature of scientific truth and the process of scientific inquiry. Includes discussion of historic cases of scientific fraud.

(3)
THE NORMATIVE structure of science
Merton, R K
In: The sociology of science: theoretical and empirical investigations, edited by N W
    Storer
    University of Chicago Press, 1973 pp267-78
A classic work on the sociology of science originally published as Science and Technology in a Democratic Order (*Journal of Legal and Political Sociology*, 1942 volume 1 pp115-26). Identifies cognitive (technical) and moral (social) norms of the scientific endeavour, the latter consisting of universalism, communality, disinterestedness and organised scepticism. This 605pp compilation of Merton's papers includes many other examples of his thinking on the nature of science and scientific advance.

(4)
AGAINST method: outline of an anarchistic theory of knowledge
Feyerabend, P
NLB: London, 1975. 339pp

Describes science as an essentially anarchistic enterprise in which progress can be made on the basis of traditional experimentation and verification, or as the result of complete chance. Uses historical examples, including that of Galileo, to argue the case that 'reason cannot be universal and unreason cannot be excluded'.

(5)
DEVIANT behavior and social control in science
Zuckerman, H
In: Deviance and social change, edited by E Sagarin
   Sage: Beverly Hills, 1977 pp87-138
A comprehensive review from the Mertonian school which sees the scientific system as self-correcting, and scientific deception as a rare anomaly. For more from Harriet Zuckerman
See also: Norms and deviant behavior in science, by H Zuckerman (Science, Technology and Human Values, 1984 9(1) pp7-13)

(6)
THE ETHICS of science
Mohr, M
Interdisciplinary Science Reviews, 1979 4(1) pp45-53
Argues that science is subject to strong social controls derived from its intrinsic value system. Looks at why scientists accept this normative code as compulsory, and discusses whether it can be formulated in explicit terms for use in day-to-day work. Also discusses whether the ethics of science could be extended to society at large. Concludes that a re-establishment of the ethical code of science is essential to restore public confidence in the trustworthiness of the natural sciences.

(7)
FRAUD in science
Weinstein, D
Social Science Quarterly, Mar 1979 59(4) pp639-52, 31 references
Reviews the increasing interest in scientific fraud following the Summerlin and Burt cases before examining the Mertonian norms of science. Looks at conditions for the erosion of normative controls, barriers to their enforcement, and the consequences of fraud in science. Argues that the existing policing of fraud is ineffective or non-existent because scientific specialisation makes it essential, in practical terms, for scientists to trust to the honesty of their colleagues. There are also barriers to replication of experiments which is poorly rewarded, lacks status and may disrupt friendships and professional relationships.

(8)
THE PUBLIC and science policy
Prewitt, K
Science, Technology and Human Values, Spring 1982 7(1) pp5-14
Contrasts the ethos of science with its emphasis on internalised standards, peer control and professional autonomy with the ethos of liberal democracy which focuses on public scrutiny, control and accountability. For another article, and subsequent commentaries, on a similar theme
See also: The life sciences and the public: is science too important to be left to the scientist, by M L Goggin (Politics and the Life Sciences, Aug 1984 3(1) pp28-75, 141 references)

(9)
A SOCIOLOGICAL approach to fraud in science
Bridgstock, M
Australian and New Zealand Journal of Sociology, Nov 1982 18(3) pp364-83,
72 references
Applies sociological theory to the issue of scientific fraud using both systems and action approaches. The first shows that there are areas in science, and on its periphery, in which social controls inhibiting misconduct do not operate. Within mainstream science there is the additional problem of the lack of guaranteed detection. The action approach indicates possible motivating factors for fraudulent behaviour including a strong commitment to a particular theory, career considerations, and political views.

(10)
OPEN information and secrecy in research
Faberge, A C
Perspectives in Biology and Medicine, Winter 1982 25(2) pp263-78
Scientific reporting may not always be an accurate reflection of actual research practice, an issue which is becoming more and more important in the context of conflicts of interest, academic–industry links and the pressure to preserve intellectual property.

(11)
FRAUD in science
Altman, L and Melcher, L
British Medical Journal, 25 Jun 1983 286(6383) pp2003-06, 17 references
Cases such as that involving cardiologist John Darsee have focused attention on the incidence of fraud in scientific research, and the willingness of the scientific establishment to confront it. There is no consensus about how widespread deception is, whether it can be identified and controlled through traditional peer review methods, or whether it should be a matter of public concern.

(12)
FRAUD and the norms of human science
Schmaus, W
Science, Technology and Human Values, Fall 1983 8(4) pp12-22, 48 notes and references
Looks at the Mertonian norms of science, as developed by Harriet Zuckerman, and discusses the policy implications of scientific misconduct. Argues that the growth of scientific knowledge does not depend on a unique commitment to disinterestedness and that it is unfair to expect scientists to follow a different moral code from everyone else. The pursuit of scientific knowledge is not so important as a moral value that it overrides the scientist's right to pursue his or her career. Thus scientists who cheat betray a common moral rule, not one which is peculiar to science. For further comment from Warren Schmaus
See also: Fraud and negligence in science, by W Schmaus (Connecticut Medicine, Mar 1983 47(3) pp155-58, 22 notes and references)

(13)
RESEARCH misconduct: an issue of science policy and practice
Chubin, D E
National Science Foundation, 1800 G Street NW, Washington, DC 20550, 1984.
The final report of the Ethics and Values in Science and Technology Program. Analyses

the causes and consequences of research malpractice, and the stages in the scientific process at which it can occur. Includes comment on several well known cases, and concludes by looking at the control of misconduct at the laboratory, institutional and governmental levels. For summary and comment by Daryl Chubin
See also: Misconduct in research: an issue of science policy and practice, by D E Chubin (Minerva, Summer 1985 23(2) pp175-202, 123 notes and references)
Research malpractice, by D E Chubin (BioScience, Feb 1985 35(2) pp80-89, 53 references)

(14)
EXPLORING the compromise of ethical principles in science
Knight, J A
Perspectives in Biology and Medicine, Spring 1984 27(3) pp432-42
Describes the ideal scientific personality as honest, open and in pursuit of truth. However, history is littered with evidence of lapses from this high standard. Looks at the attitudes and values of scientists in the biomedical field.

(15)
AN INTRODUCTION to science studies: the philosophical and social aspects of science and technology
Ziman, J
Cambridge University Press, 1984. 203pp
A broad overview of the philosophy, sociology, psychology and politics of science and technology. For more up to date views from John Ziman and Andrew Webster on the increasingly complex interrelationships between science, the economy, society and politics
See also: Prometheus bound: science in a dynamic steady state, by J Ziman (Cambridge University Press, May 1994. 289pp)
Of one mind: the collectivization of science, by J Ziman (American Institute of Physics Press, 1995. 407pp)
Science, technology and society: new directions, by A Webster (Macmillan: Basingstoke, 1992. 212pp)

(16)
FORGING, cooking, trimming, and riding on the bandwagon
Franklin, A
American Journal of Physics, Sep 1984 52(9) pp786-93, 86 references
Explores the degree to which experimental replication can be regarded as an adequate safeguard against scientific fraud, using evidence from four cases involving physics research. Concludes that the system works effectively, especially in the context of experiments of theoretical importance.

(17)
DEVIANT scientist and scientific deviance
Bechtel, H K and Pearson, W
Deviant Behavior, 1985 6(3) pp237-52
Discusses fraud in the form of data fabrication and manipulation by scientists, practices which are supposed to be prevented by the normative structure of science. Looks at ways of explaining this allegedly atypical behaviour using contributions from anomie, interactionist and conflict theories.

(18)
PROMETHEUS the impostor
Laor, N
British Medical Journal, 2 Mar 1985 290(6469) pp681-84, 19 references
A critique of attacks on science (Prometheus) which argue that the process of scientific inquiry encourages dishonesty. Challenges the assumptions of William Broad and Nicholas Wade in *Betrayers of the truth* (Ref. 69, Ch. 2), and of three influential philosophers who have written about error and deceit: Francis Bacon, Paul K Feyerabend and Thomas Kuhn. Endorses Karl Popper's view of the scientific method as the creation of progress from the identification of error, and calls on the scientific community to recognise the inevitability of human fallibility.

(19)
SCIENTIFIC fraud: social deviance or the failure of virtue?
List, C J
Science, Technology and Human Values, Fall 1985 10(4) pp27-36, 48 notes and references
Defines scientific fraud as a strategy designed to increase the chances of success in the competition for external rewards. Given the evolutionary nature of science, norms (cognitive or moral) are insufficient to detect or deter fraud. At the same time, the problem must be addressed because fraud undercuts the very essence of science. Argues that the key lies in re-establishing the importance of internal rewards (such as intellectual satisfaction) as against the external ones of money, fame etc.

(20)
DEVIANCE in science
Ben-Yehuda, N
British Journal of Criminology, Jan 1986 26(1) pp1-27, 94 references
Outlines the Mertonian social controls on science (communality, organised scepticism, replication) but notes that there is little formal policing in science and a very high reliance on trust. Examines the forces conducive to deviance including loss of communality (secrecy for commercial reasons, lags in the dissemination of information); failures of the replication process; the low probability of being found out; and the lack of effective sanctions if one is caught. Added to this are positive factors promoting deviance such as the pressure to publish. Personality factors are of limited relevance. Fraud occurs because social controls are weak and because elements of the scientific system are productive of deviant behaviour.

(21)
DIAMOND dealers and feather merchants: tales from the sciences
Klotz, I M
Birkhauser: Boston, 1986. 120pp
A lively account of historic cases of scientific self-deception. For an analysis of the polywater story, one of the more entertaining instances of scientific credulity
See also: Polywater, by F Franks (MIT Press, 1981. 208pp)

(22)
FRAUD, fakery and fudging: behavior analysis and bad science
Blakely, E and others
In: Research methods in applied behavior analysis: issues and advances, edited by A Poling and R W F Fuqua
Plenum Press: New York, 1986 pp313-30, 44 references

An historical review of scientific fraud going back to Ptolemy and including comment on the dubious work of Levy in parapsychology; the wishful thinking of French scientists over the existence, or otherwise, of N-rays in the early 1900s; the fraudulent work of the Sobells in treating alcoholics; and Mark Spector's fraudulent cancer research. Argues that, like the poor, fraudsters are always with us. Discusses the motivations for, and consequences of, fraud drawing attention to weaknesses in government research grant procedures and peer review. Also comments briefly on the 'whistleblower effect'.

(23)
FALSE data and last hopes: enrolling ineligible patients in clinical trials
Vanderpool, H Y and Weiss, G B
Hastings Center Report, Apr 1987 17(2) pp16-19, 5 references
Looks at the potential conflict between an individual patient's best interests and the principles of scientific methodology. Such a conflict may, in the case of cancer research discussed here, lead a doctor to falsify data in order to enrol a dying patient in the trial of a new drug which may be his or her only chance of survival. For further discussion of the ethical dilemmas that can face biomedical researchers in their relationships with human subjects
See also: The case for deception in medical experimentation, by J D Newell (In: Ethical issues in scientific research: an anthology, edited by E Erwin and others. Garland Publishing: London, 1994 pp141-53)

(24)
WHAT do we know about fraud and other forms of intellectual dishonesty in science? Part 1: the spectrum of deviant behaviour in science
Garfield, E
Current Contents: Clinical Medicine, 6 Apr 1987 15(14) pp3-7, 41 references
Discusses the range of behaviours encountered in attempts to define scientific fraud using information gained from an examination of the Institute of Scientific Information's databases. Describes much of the 'evidence' as informal or anecdotal rather than based on rigorous, controlled studies.

(25)
WHAT do we know about fraud and other forms of intellectual dishonesty in science? Part 2: why does fraud happen and what are its effects?
Garfield, E
Current Contents: Clinical Medicine, 13 Apr 1987 15(15) pp3-10, 57 references
Part 2 focuses on explanations of the causes of such behaviour, and the actions being taken, or discussed, to deal with it.

(26)
DECEPTION in scientific research
Woolf, P K
Jurimetrics Journal, Fall 1988 29(1) pp67-95, 55 notes and references
Reviews the findings of the Congressional Committee on Science and Technology, Subcommittee on Investigations and Oversight (chaired by Al Gore) on the dramatic increase in allegations of scientific fraud in the USA in the 1970s and early 1980s (Ref. 138, Ch. 3). Looks at whether the cases were anomalies, as the scientific community contended, or the tip of an iceberg, and whether universities and federal agencies were effective in detecting and resolving cases. The research community successfully maintained its stance that misconduct was rare, and no action was taken as a result of the Subcommittee's work.

(27)
SCIENCE, technology and society: emerging relationships
Chalk, R (editor)
American Association for the Advancement of Science, 1333 H Street, Washington DC 20005, 1988. 262pp
A useful compilation of articles published in the journal *Science* between 1949 and 1988 on issues such as ethics, scientific freedom and scientific responsibility.

(28)
PRINCIPLES of biomedical ethics: 3rd edition
Beauchamp, T L and Childress, J F
Oxford University Press: New York, 1989. 470pp
An influential work in the United States which defines four fundamental ethical principles: autonomy, nonmaleficence, beneficence and justice. These were adopted by the President's Commission for the Study of Ethical Problems in Medicine and Biomedical and Behavioral Research. For a brief selection of more recent American analyses of ethical issues in science which include comment on scientific deception and misconduct
See also: The ethical dimensions of the biological sciences, by R E Bulger and others (Cambridge University Press: New York, 1993. 294pp, references)
Ethical issues in research, by D Cheney (University Publishing Group: Frederick, MD, 1993. 237pp)
Ethical issues in scientific research: an anthology, edited by E Erwin and others (Garland Publishing: London, 1994. 416pp)
Research ethics: cases and materials, edited by R L Penslar (Indiana University Press: Bloomington, IN, 1994. 278pp)
Ethics of scientific research, by K Shrader-Frechette (Rowman and Littlefield: Lanham, MD, Sep 1994. 208pp)
Society's choices: social and ethical decision making in biomedicine, edited by R E Bulger and others (National Academy Press: Washington, DC, 1995. 541pp)

(29)
ACCEPTED practices? A view from outside
Dubois, B-L
Perspectives in Biology and Medicine, Summer 1989 32(4) pp605-12, 27 references
Reviews trends in misconduct in the USA, focusing on the reporting of research – multiple publication, co-authorship etc. Also comments on definitional problems, calling on the scientific community to consider a wider (not narrower) spectrum of problematic ethical situations to determine actual, as opposed to accepted, practices.

(30)
UNDERREPORTING research is scientific misconduct
Chalmers, I
Journal of the American Medical Association, 9 Mar 1990 263(10) pp1405-08, 38 references
Discusses the practice of failing to publish non-confirmatory data altogether, or to publish only those portions of the evidence which substantiate the clinical or experimental hypothesis. Argues that this may be much more prevalent than the deliberate falsification of data, and can be attributed in part to the pressure on scientists to publish positive results. Looks at ways the problem can be overcome.

(31)
DECEIT in science: does it really matter?
A J Birch
Interdisciplinary Science Reviews, Dec 1990 15(4) pp334-43, 12 references
Looks at how misconduct and deceit occurs, arguing that although it may not have a
serious long term effect on the expansion of knowledge, it matters because 'it is a sin
against humanity and a contradiction of the whole ethical basis of science'. Scientific
establishments should be readier to confront the problem.

(32)
MAKING science: between nature and society
Cole, S
Harvard University Press: Cambridge, MA, 1992. 290pp
Analyses and criticises more modern (post-Merton) thinking on the sociology of science.
Also includes a critique of the National Science Foundation peer review system. For a
defence of this, which argues that NSF peer review has 'generally served well to ensure
effectiveness and efficiency in decisionmaking in research projects'
See also: Major award decisionmaking at the National Science Foundation (National
Academy Press: Washington, DC, 1994. 160pp)

(33)
MISCONDUCT and fraud in the empirical sciences: history and overview
Miller, D J and Hersen, M
In: Research fraud in the behavioral and biomedical sciences, edited by
    D J Miller and M Hersen
    Wiley: Chichester, 1992 pp3-16
A useful review of developments in thinking on the nature of science and scientific
deviance. The subsequent chapter, Ethics and the Nature of Empirical Science, by K F
Schaffner (pp17-33) discusses the norms, values and ethics of science.

(34)
THE SCIENTIFIC attitude: 2nd edition
Grinnell, F
Westview Press: Boulder, CO, 1992. 141pp, bibliography
Originally published in 1987. Chapter 2 deals with scientific misconduct.

(35)
SCIENTIFIC literacy and the myth of scientific method
Bauer, H H
University of Illinois Press, 1992. 192pp
Attacks the conventional arguments in favour of broadening the scientific literacy of the
public, especially the claims that scientific knowledge is different, and more important,
than other types of knowledge. Argues that it may be more useful for lay people to
know how science works rather than its results: for example, to appreciate that science is
not the dispassionate, systematic, objective pursuit of truth that many believe it to be.

(36)
FRAUD in science: an economic approach
Wible, J R
Philosophy of the Social Sciences, Mar 1992 22(1) pp5-27, 65 notes and references
Argues that there is no coherent framework for analysing the fraud issue, and
recommends the use of economic analysis. This produces two categories of misconduct:
replication failure and fraud. The former is best understood as a scientist making optimal

use of time in an environment where innovation rather than replication is emphasised. The latter is understood as a deliberate gamble in which the scientist takes advantage of the inherent uncertainty and complexity of science (and undermines its integrity) for personal gain or advancement.

(37)
MISTAKES and fraud in medical research
Friedman, P J
Law, Medicine and Health Care, Spring/Summer 1992 20(1/2) pp17-25
Looks at the implications of a growing number of reported frauds in biomedical research on the consensus about the nature of research ethics. Once 'something everyone agrees about', it is now the subject of considerable disagreement. Distinguishing between error and fraud is no longer as obvious, or as easy, as it used to seem.

(38)
SCIENTIFIC fraud and the power structure of science
Martin, B
Prometheus, Jun 1992 10(1) pp83-98
Discusses this issue in the Australian context, noting how the restrictive definitions of fraud adopted by the scientific establishment and powerful government and corporate elites distract attention from other undesirable aspects of scientific behaviour.

(39)
THE DEFINITION of misconduct in science: a view from NSF
Buzzelli, D E
Science, 29 Jan 1993 259(5095) pp584-85, 647-48
Comments on the implications of the National Science Foundation's open-ended definition of misconduct which includes the phrase 'other serious deviations from accepted practices'. Although this has worked quite successfully, and enables the NSF to take action on cases which do not fall into the usual lists of types of misconduct (including misuse of funds, sexual harassment and vandalism), there is also the possibility of abuse. For additional comment on the continuing debate for and against open-ended definitions
See also: Divisive dispute smolders over definition of scientific misconduct, by P S Zurer (Chemical and Engineering News, 5 Apr 1993 71(14) pp23-25)

(40)
DEFINING scientific misconduct: the relevance of mental state
Dresser, R
Journal of the American Medical Association, 17 Feb 1993 269(7) pp895-97,
39 references
Devising and implementing a fair system of policing scientific deception is dependent on the development of precise and appropriate definitions of unacceptable behaviour. This is an essential precursor to progress in resolving many other difficult issues including the required degree of due process protection for accused persons, the nature of adjudication procedures and the range of acceptable sanctions which might be imposed on wrongdoers.

(41)
WHAT is scientific misconduct?
Bridgstock, M
Search, Apr 1993 24(3) pp75-78

Interviews with 30 Australian scientists show that there is a strong consensus on the reprehensible nature of data falsification and plagiarism. However, there is substantial disagreement over whether publicity-seeking, heavy self-citation and the omission of anomalous results can be classified as misconduct.

(42)

WHAT is misconduct in science?
Schachman, H K
Science, 9 Jul 1993 261(5118) pp148-49, 183, 15 notes and references
Discusses the implications of the open-ended definitions of scientific misconduct used by the National Science Foundation and National Institutes of Health, arguing that they make it difficult 'to distinguish between the crooks and the jerks'. Looks at the evolution of definitions in the USA since the early 1980s, and calls for a much more rigorous approach. Highly critical of Buzzelli's support for open-ended definitions (see Ref. 39 above).

(43)

A NEW perspective on scientific misconduct
Hackett, E J
Academic Medicine, Sep 1993 68(9) ppS72-S76, 21 references
Increasing social concern about scientific misconduct is indicative of a changing relationship between science and society in which the former is increasingly important as a source of economic and other kinds of power. As a result, there is an increased propensity for outside intervention and scrutiny. Looks at ways in which the relationship between science and society can be re-negotiated to alleviate the 'pathogenic pressures' in the present environment.

(44)

PROCESS and detection in fraud and deceit
Silverman, S
Ethics and Behavior, 1994 4(3) pp219-28, 16 references
Argues that very little has been written on the process of fraud, as opposed to specific cases, and that a better understanding could help improve detection procedures and policy responses. Develops such an understanding on the basis of an analysis of several cases studies from diverse fields, and the derivation of general principles about the process of fraud.

(45)

THE MURKY borderland between scientific intuition and fraud
Segerstrale, U
In: Ethical issues in scientific research: an anthology, edited by E Erwin and others
    Garland Publishing: London, 1994 pp91-109, 17 notes and references
Argues that scientific fraud and the fudging of data may not be the clear cut issue it appears to be. 'Good' science is difficult to describe explicitly because it includes an element of intuition and tacit knowledge. This may sometimes shade into deception in pursuit of a theory which a scientist *knows* is right (or wrong) despite 'objective' evidence. Looks at how 'good' science can be promoted, arguing that education in proper scientific method should start very young,

(46)

FORBIDDEN science: suppressed research that could change our lives
Milton, R
Fourth Estate: London, Apr 1994. 264pp

A science journalist explores the ways in which large scale, orthodox science allegedly suppresses small scale, unorthodox but sometimes potentially very valuable research. Uses historical examples to show how science which is now taken for granted was once ridiculed, and argues that the scientific establishment is still hostile to 'the oxygen of eccentricity'. For a more academic analysis of 'deviant' science
See also: On the margins of science: the social construction of rejected knowledge, edited by R Wallis (University of Keele, 1979. 337pp. Sociological Review Monograph 27)

(47)
MISCONDUCT in science: should its definition include mischievous or improper allegations?
Burgman, M A
Quarterly Review of Biology, Jun 1994 69(2) pp233-35, 12 references
Argues that the debate on scientific misconduct should include a recognition of the fact that some individuals may make accusations in bad faith, possibly to sabotage the research work of competitors. This does not, however, absolve societies from developing proper systems of protection for whistleblowers. Focuses particularly on what Burgman considers to be the improper airing of instances of alleged misconduct by B Müller-Hill, a German researcher
See also: Science, truth and other values, by B Müller-Hill (Quarterly Review of Biology, Sep 1993 68(3) pp399-407)

(48)
THE BETRAYERS
Millson, P (editor)
The Betrayers, PO Box 7, London W3 6XJ, Mar 1995. 13pp
Edited transcript of a programme in the BBC *Horizon* series which examines the issue of scientific deception in the biomedical field.

(49)
WHO'S holding the moral high ground?
Postgate, J
New Scientist, 8 Apr 1995 146(1972) pp45-46
Describes science as neutral, and the practice of science as morally superior because of the 'stern morality' imposed on scientists by the search for the truth.

(50)
CONDUCT in science
Science, 23 Jun 1995 268(5218) pp1706-18
A special feature examining the 'grey' areas of scientific conduct – practices which fall short of outright fraud and which are prompted by the increasing competitiveness of the scientific endeavour. Editorial comment (p1679) argues that these 'other misdeeds, more subtle and more common...can do far greater damage to the fabric of scientific inquiry'. Articles discuss the issue of individual credit for scientific work, which is placing great strain on the culture of collaboration and free exchange of information and research materials; authorship; and the development of programmes in American universities to teach the ethical conduct of science. *Science* is planning to foster an 'ongoing discussion' of the issues through the Internet. The American Association for the Advancement of Science home page is at URL:http://www.aaas.org: call up the Beyond the Printed Page section of the *Science* home page.

2. THE PRESSURES ON SCIENTISTS

2.1 The prevalence of deception

Any attempt to put a figure on the prevalence of deception in science is bedevilled by the lack of objective evidence, and by the scientific establishment's insistence that it is an isolated and rare phenomenon. While the existence of increasing pressures on scientists is freely admitted, and is a source of much criticism of government policies, it is rare for an explicit connection to be made between such pressures and everyday behaviour at the laboratory bench. Although analyses of the scientific process suggest that deception covers a broad spectrum of activities, attention has been concentrated on the rare cases of gross fraud which often serve to confirm the scientific community's belief in psychological disturbance as the main cause of such behaviour. Considerable effort has been expended in the development of legalistic definitions of misconduct which can then be isolated from the rest of the scientific process.

The problem with this approach is that it diverts attention from those other everyday behaviours which may be less obviously reprehensible than outright falsification or plagiarism but could have an equally damaging effect both on science and the public good. As Chapter 1 suggests, many of these might be classified as rational (or at least human) responses to the situations imposed on scientists by government and the organisations they work for – the pressure to deliver the right results at the right time, to keep costs down, to win the next research grant, or to extend a temporary contract of employment.

It is understandable that most scientists react cautiously to apparent evidence of misconduct given the inherent difficulties of distinguishing between error and deliberate deception in a complex research environment. However, there are other characteristics of the scientific world which can work in favour of this kind of diffidence. Among the most influential is the general reluctance to believe that members of the scientific community deliberately breach ethical norms, a characteristic which science shares with many other professions governed by strict codes of conduct. Alexander Kohn, in his book *False prophets*, expressed it thus – 'unlike other professions where honesty is merely regarded as highly desirable, the whole edifice of science is built upon honesty' and, one might add, the presumption of honesty in others. Accusations of deception challenge the very basis of the scientist's self-image as a bastion of objectivity and truth in an irrational world (Ref. 66).

Closing ranks

A common reflection of this belief is a tendency to close ranks in support of accused members, to give them the benefit of the doubt, and (allegedly) to sweep evidence under the carpet if at all possible. The adoption of highly restrictive definitions of what constitutes misconduct is only one of several approaches designed, no doubt unconsciously, to protect the image of science from contamination. Others include attempts to confine the problem to particular areas of research – principally biomedicine – which are described as somehow different from the rest of science and more likely to foster deceptive behaviour.

An American analysis of whistleblowing in biomedical research published in 1981 (Ref. 139, Ch. 3) includes arguments which are typical of this effort to prove that deceivers are 'not one of us' and never have been. The authors contrast the values of 'real' scientists in the biomedical field with those who have entered research after training as doctors. The doctor's primary ethic is concerned with the well-being of patients, not the pursuit of scientific truth, and this could easily influence his or her work in the research environment. Moreover, the highly competitive nature of pre-medical training in the USA is said to foster dishonesty among undergraduates which, again, may contaminate the purity of the 'real' scientific endeavour at a later stage. Finally, biomedicine is said to be unique in terms of competitive pressures and potential rewards which may be conducive to deceptive behaviour by these already ethically compromised doctor-scientists.

This analysis is superficially attractive given the fact that such a high proportion of exposed misconduct cases concern the biomedical sciences. However, the apparently higher incidence of deceptive behaviour in this field may equally well be a product of greater openness in comparison with other disciplines, the more effective operation of self-correcting mechanisms such as peer review, or greater public and political interest in the activities of this particular group of scientists. In the absence of objective comparative data it is impossible to tell. However, it is certainly not the case that biomedicine has a monopoly on unethical behaviour. There have been cases in psychology, archaeology, chemistry, physics, engineering, environmental science and other fields.

Other diversionary tactics employed by the scientific community include the denial of deception as a major problem, and its downgrading to a 'moral mischief'. This line of argument states that fraud is trivial because it is not genuine science and cannot, therefore, have any long term impact. In the words of one senior American scientist such cases are 'amusing, and they have an interesting human element to them but...these incidents represent small tempests in a teapot and are soon glossed over. One soon finds out what the real answers are and forgets these minor impediments which happened along the way'.

Unfortunately this comforting analysis ignores the quite understandable propensity of scientists to take colleagues at their word, and the resultant possibility that they might be deceived into absorbing untruths into the canon of 'normal' science, if only for a period. Peer review and replication – the self-correcting mechanisms of science – have largely failed to detect the grosser frauds of recent years and it is no longer safe to say that deception does not matter, if only because its impact on the research literature may persist even after its exposure.

The conventional view

The scientific community's reluctance to confront the possibility of deception publicly, and its tendency to exclude all but the grossest misconduct from detailed investigation, may well lie behind the discrepancies which exist between the conventional view of deception as a rare problem and survey data which suggest that it may be much more widespread. The former view is well represented in the literature from Charles Babbage onwards. In his *Reflections on the decline of science in England, and on some of its causes*, published in 1830, he accepted that fraud was a potential problem, but a rare one. 'The cook [the scientist] would procure a temporary reputation...at the expense of his permanent fame', presumably because the self-correcting mechanisms of science would inevitably find him out (Ref. 51).

Many more modern observers are equally convinced that science is well able to police itself, and that the vast majority of scientists adhere to a strict ethical code. Robert K Merton in his analysis of *The normative structure of science* (Ref. 3, Ch. 1) reported a 'virtual absence of fraud in the annals of science'. William Broad and Nicholas Wade, in their study of *Betrayers of the truth,* claimed that there were only 34 cases of proven or highly suspected fraud between the second century AD and the early 1980s, although they quoted these figures in support of their view that publicly exposed cases are only the tip of the fraud iceberg (Ref. 69).

This assertion led to a predictable storm of protest from the scientific community, as have many other similar claims. Few issues unite scientists so strongly as their distaste for the media, and many are convinced that its treatment of scientific misconduct is both irresponsible and sensationalist. There is, no doubt, an element of truth in this belief when it relates to the mass media with its tendency to oversimplify in the interests of selling a story to a non-scientific public. However, writers like Broad and Wade, who are very experienced science journalists working for the specialist press, cannot be treated in the same way. Nor can equally controversial analysts like Beth Savan who is both a journalist and an environmental consultant with a doctorate in ecology.

Despite growing concerns among well-informed commentators, the public and politicians about the prevalence of deception, the scientific establishment in the United States persisted in its claims that the problem was minor. In an often-quoted *Science* editorial of the late 1980s, Daniel Koshland claimed that '99.9999% of reports are accurate and truthful' (Ref. 57), while analyses in the 1980s of misconduct in research funded by the US National Institutes of Health (which was facing an increase in reported cases at the time) suggested that the problem was 'almost insignificant' in the context of science as a whole (Refs. 54, 56). Similarly, many of the guidance documents listed in the next chapter begin by stating that the problem they address is uncommon, though naturally serious.

Survey evidence

However, when practising scientists are asked to report their experiences anonymously, the picture is rather different although the amount and quality of the data are both limited. These deficiencies have, as already noted, allowed the scientific establishment to dismiss the findings of surveys as unrepresentative or invalid because they relate to perceptions rather than proven fact. Published data from the UK and Europe are particularly sparse. In 1976 *New Scientist* conducted a survey of its readers in the wake of the Cyril Burt affair and received 201 valid replies. Of these, 194 reported knowledge of cheating, with 20% of the perpetrators caught in the act, usually of manipulating data rather than outright falsification. Perhaps most interestingly, only 10% of those caught were dismissed (Ref. 52).

In 1988 the then editor of the *British Medical Journal*, Stephen Lock, published the results of a small scale and non-systematic survey of 80 scientists. Over half knew of some instance of misconduct, and in over half the cases fraudulent or dubious results had been published in the literature. Only six retractions had subsequently appeared, apparently 'too vague to indicate what had gone on'. Nor did perpetrators appear to have been formally disciplined, with only one suffering dismissal. These findings were instrumental in the build up of pressure in the UK for a concerted response to a problem, the existence of which the scientific community, research institutions and policy makers seemed almost totally unwilling to admit (Ref. 61).

Further evidence from Norway, based on data collected over the period 1986-1992 from 119 scientists, shows a similar conflict between the conventional view of deception as a rare problem and scientific opinion as expressed in surveys. Some 40% claimed that fraud was a problem in Norway (although 46% argued that it was less so than in other countries); 27% knew of one or more cases of misconduct, with 42% stating that their knowledge was not publicly known; and 18% claimed to have been personally exposed to misconduct. Over half felt that better procedures were needed to investigate allegations and prosecute in the event of confirmed misconduct. Perhaps the most interesting evidence in this and other surveys is the juxtaposition between the respondents' knowledge or direct experience of deception and their willingness to take active steps to challenge it (Ref. 70).

Evidence from the United States is rather more plentiful. In 1987 *New Scientist* published the results of a further survey, this time of researchers at a large American university, showing that 32% suspected a colleague of falsifying data, and a further 32% suspected a colleague of plagiarism (Ref. 59). However, fewer than half took steps to verify their suspicions of serious deception, let alone action to remedy the situation. At around the same time an analysis of data audits carried out by the US Food and Drug Administration between 1977 and 1988 suggested that there were serious deficiencies in 12% of the audits conducted before 1985. The rate declined to 7% after that date, suggesting that data audits may have an important role to play in reducing the incidence of deception and sloppy research practice in investigational drug trials (Ref. 62). This seems to be confirmed by an analysis of audits carried out at a group of institutions participating in the Cancer and Leukemia Group B (Ref. 74).

In 1989 the Society of University Surgeons carried out a survey of its active members, asking for opinions on the nature, incidence and reduction of fraud. Just over 200 (82% of those polled) replied. Forty per cent of members were aware of at least one incident of fraud that had been openly investigated by their institution, and 43% were aware of at least one 'quiet' inquiry. Nearly 30% had directly refuted data published by a colleague, while 15% strongly suspected that uninvestigated fraud existed in their institutions, this despite the fact that 75% had published science-related ethics policies. The vast majority of respondents favoured severe academic penalties for scientists who cheat, believing that the unethical conduct of a few, penalises honest researchers. Interestingly, given the alleged reluctance of the scientific community to admit the possibility of fraud, the members of the Society were quite clear that it is not a new problem. Moreover, they accepted that existing safeguards within the academic and scientific publishing worlds are insufficient to prevent it (Ref. 64).

Among the most recent data are the findings of a member opinion poll carried out by the American Association for the Advancement of Science and published in March 1992. Some 470 members replied (a 31% response rate), of whom 37% believed that fraud and misconduct had increased over the previous ten years; 44% believed levels had stayed the same, and most were united in condemning the media for exaggerating the problem. Nonetheless, over 50% believed that university procedures for dealing with deception were too lax, and 27% admitted having encountered or witnessed suspected fraudulent research in the previous ten years although fewer than one in four cases led to an admission or determination of wrong-doing (Ref. 67).

In a later survey published in *American Scientist* of a much larger sample of faculty members and graduate students across the USA, 9% reported direct (though not necessarily confirmed) knowledge of plagiarism, and 6% of data falsification. This analysis carried out by Judith Swazey and her colleagues also claims that other forms of unethical behaviour are much more widespread than plagiarism and data falsification. These include the exploitation of staff and discrimination against minorities, but also practices which could well be classified within the mainstream of scientific misconduct – the misuse of research funds, and lack of compliance with rules on the ethical conduct of research (Ref. 75).

Nor are deceptive and unethical practices confined to universities according to a survey published in *Science, Technology and Human Values* in early 1994. This covered nearly 1,500 members of three professional bodies in the USA that undertake risk analyses in areas such as environmental economics, epidemiology, exposure assessment and toxicology. A third of the respondents had observed biased research design, 20% had witnessed plagiarism, and 10% data falsification. They attributed these problems to poor scientific method, economic pressures and lack of training. All supported the improved teaching of ethics but, in common with their colleagues in other disciplines, were almost unanimously opposed to any government auditing of their work (Ref. 77).

Whistleblowing

In the context of prevailing disbelief and a tendency towards the cover-up, whistleblowing in science can be a dangerous and distressing business – it brings 'no applause, few rewards, and little public satisfaction' according to Marcel LaFollette (Ref. 65). For example, the hierarchical organisation of research institutions can make it difficult, if not impossible, for a junior scientist to challenge the behaviour of senior colleagues. Advancement in science, operating as it does through the peer review system, still retains many characteristics of patronage, and an ambitious young scientist might well think twice about questioning another's conduct too openly. At the same time, most scientific work involves close personal collaboration with other people, and rumours of misconduct can cause unpleasantness and disruption in the working environment. Despite a no doubt general adherence to ethical principles, scientists are only human and it is reasonable to believe that at least some of those who witness deception will prefer to turn a blind eye in the interests of a quiet life.

The experience of Margot O'Toole, whistleblower in the still unresolved 'Baltimore case', is indicative of what can happen when the conduct of colleagues is questioned. She was instrumental in exposing the publication of an allegedly fraudulent paper in the journal *Cell* by immunologist Thereza Imanishi-Kari, co-authored by Nobel laureate, David Baltimore. Although eventually vindicated in 1991 when she received a public apology from Baltimore, O'Toole took great risks as an untenured post-doctoral fellow in criticising 'prestigious and powerful scientists'. Her career was allegedly ruined in the interim and she was publicly accused of both vindictiveness and scientific incompetence (Ref. 63). In a world in which whistleblowing is often regarded as more reprehensible than the conduct it addresses, it takes considerable courage for an insider to take action.

Outsiders may find it easier, and in several of the more notorious cases exposure has been effected by what LaFollette calls nemesis figures – individuals who are prepared to risk the odium and professional obloquy which may accompany their activities in the interests of promoting the integrity of science. Walter W Stewart and Ned Feder, who first came to public attention in the 1980s through their attempts to publish an article on the honorary co-authors of disgraced cardiologist John Darsee, are classic examples (Ref. 60).

The saga began in 1983 when a first draft was submitted to *Nature*. This caused uproar among Darsee's co-authors who, while not condoning his fraudulent actions, believed that their own reputations would be unfairly damaged by publication of Stewart and Feder's analysis. Threats of legal action for libel followed, and Stewart and Feder tried unsuccessfully to get their article published elsewhere. The issue was ultimately resolved by its publication in the *Congressional Record* after the controversy was discussed by the House Committee on Science and Technology. This removed the threat of libel, and the article finally appeared in *Nature* in January 1987 (Ref. 95).

Despite this success, Stewart and Feder remain controversial figures. In 1993 they were ordered by the National Institutes of Health, where they work in the National Institute of Diabetes and Digestive and Kidney Diseases, to refrain from pursuing scientific misconduct cases 'at government expense'. They were reassigned to 'administrative duties' – Walter Stewart promptly going on hunger strike for some weeks – but continued to investigate new misconduct cases, allegedly in their own time. In early 1995 they were accused of violating the 1993 order by writing a letter on NIH stationery to the Department of Health and Human Services Commission on Research Integrity; this despite the fact that they had been given written permission to appear before the Commission (Ref. 65). Although the reprimand was quickly withdrawn, Stewart and Feder are still apparently regarded with distaste by many within the NIH as failed scientists and inveterate publicity seekers, now with their own home page on the World Wide Web (wstewart@nyx.cs.du.edu).

However, distaste for the whistleblower cannot hide the fact that deception does happen, possibly on a much wider scale than the scientific establishment is willing to admit. If the results of the few surveys carried out are to be believed, scientists can be placed under pressure in two ways: both to deceive and, if they witness deception, to keep quiet about it. This is clearly a dangerous combination. Although most scientists still manage to conduct themselves in an ethical way, a wilful refusal to believe that a significant minority might not, will blind the scientific community and policy makers to the implications of their own actions for the honourable conduct of science. It is important for both to recognise the personal and institutional factors which might induce an individual to cheat, and to respond accordingly.

(51)
REFLECTIONS on the decline of science in England, and on some of its causes
Babbage, C
Augustus Kelley: New York, 1970 pp174-83 (originally published in London in 1830, and also reprinted in Nature, 17 Aug 1989 340(6234) pp499-502)
In this section of his work, Babbage identifies three kinds of deception, claiming that all are rare: forging (falsification of data, plagiarism); trimming (manipulation of data to make them look better); and cooking (choosing only those data which fit a pre-conceived research hypothesis).

(52)
CHEATING in science
I Saint James-Roberts
New Scientist, 26 Nov 1976 72(1028) pp466-69
Presents the results of a survey of readers which suggest a high incidence of deceptive

behaviour in the laboratory. Interestingly, 45% of the cases involved more than one perpetrator, with 15% having at least three collaborators. For an introduction to the survey and a copy of the questionnaire
See also: Are researchers trustworthy? by I Saint James-Roberts (New Scientist, 2 Sep 1976 71(1016) pp481-83)

(53)
FRAUD in science: how much, how serious?
Woolf, P
Hastings Center Report, Oct 1981 11(5) pp9-14, 27 notes and references
Looks at the increasing political and public interest in scientific fraud in the USA during the early 1980s, noting that the scientific community is reluctant to acknowledge misconduct as a widespread or important problem. This 'sanguine version of collegial virtue' is no longer tenable, and the problem needs serious attention.

(54)
PHS perspectives on misconduct in science
Brandt, E T
Public Health Reports, Mar/Apr 1983 98(2) pp136-39
Shows that, between 1980 and 1982, the US National Institutes of Health was notified of 45 allegations of misconduct. This is described as a miniscule fraction in relation to the 20,000+ grants and contracts issued by NIH each year. However, by the summer of 1983 the level of allegations received by NIH was running at two a month. Half of these warranted investigation. For comment
See also: Too good to be true, by G H Cole (Harvard Magazine, Jul/Aug 1983 pp22-28)

(55)
SCIENTIFIC misconduct in investigational drug trials
Shapiro, M F and Charrow, R P
New England Journal of Medicine, 14 Mar 1984 312(11) pp731-36, 3 references
Presents data from a study of administrative procedures used by the US Food and Drug Administration in auditing research records. Finds that the work of 6.3% of audited researchers contained serious, but remediable, deficiencies, and that 5.2% showed deficiencies warranting disciplinary action. Violations included misrepresented or falsified data, non-adherence to protocols, and lack of informed consent. Later comment on FDA data audits is listed below at Ref. 62.

(56)
CURRENT NIH perspectives on misconduct in science
Miers, M L
American Psychologist, Jul 1985 40(7) pp831-35, 11 references
States the National Institutes of Health position which is still insistent that misconduct is 'almost insignificant' although the incidence of allegations has increased dramatically. However, changes in procedures and policies have been instituted. For an NIH literature search on the misconduct problem from this period, which includes 450 references
See also: Misconduct and fraud in the life sciences: January 1977 through September 1987, by J van de Kamp and M Cummings (National Institutes of Health: Bethesda, MD 20892, 1987. 17pp)

(57)

FRAUD in science

Koshland, D E

Science, 9 Jan 1987 235(4785) p141

An editorial often quoted by those who claim that deliberate deception is a rare problem. Argues that 99.9999% of all research papers are accurate and truthful.

(58)

MISCONDUCT in research: may it be more widespread than chemists like to think?

Zurer, P S

Chemical and Engineering News, 13 Apr 1987 65(15) pp10-17

Discusses this issue in the context of the case of chemistry professor, Ronald Breslow, who was forced to withdraw three communications from the *Journal of the American Chemical Society* because his research could not be fully reproduced. As in the biomedical field, there is a polarisation of opinion within chemistry between those who claim that misconduct is very rare, and those who say 'there, but for the grace of God, go I'. This editorial comment led to 16 letters (some of protest) in subsequent issues of the journal from, among others, Breslow and his graduate student co-author.

(59)

FRAUD will out – or will it? Scientists' attitudes to bogus research

Tangney, J P

New Scientist, 6 Aug 1987 115(1572) pp62-63

Presents data from a study of researchers at a large American university, showing significant levels of suspected data falsification and plagiarism but little enthusiasm for investigating and remedying it.

(60)

ALLOCATING credit and blame in science

Chubin, D E

Science, Technology and Human Values, Winter/Spring 1988 13(1/2) pp53-63, 29 references

Tells the story behind the long campaign by Walter W Stewart and Ned Feder to get their analysis of John Darsee's co-authors published in *Nature*. For more comment on their activities

See also: New censors in the academy: two approaches to curb their influence, by R D Davis (Science, Technology and Human Values, Winter/Spring 1988 13(1/2) pp64-74, 24 notes and references)

A bitter battle over error, by B J Culliton (Science, 24 Jun 1988 240(4860) pp1720-23; 1 Jul 1988 241(4861) pp18-21)

(61)

MISCONDUCT in medical research: does it exist in Britain?

Lock, S

British Medical Journal, 10 Dec 1988 287(6662) pp1531-35, 34 references

Presents the results of a non-systematic survey of 80 scientists on the incidence of plagiarism, misrepresentation and other types of misconduct. They suggest that the problem is considerably larger than generally recognised, and urges action by individual institutions, professional bodies and local ethics committees strengthened by legal representatives. For another editorial by Stephen Lock

See also: Fraud in medicine, by S Lock (British Medical Journal, 6 Feb 1988 296(6619) pp376-77, 15 references)

(62)
THE ROLE of data audits in detecting scientific misconduct
Shapiro, M F and Charrow, R P
Journal of the American Medical Association, 5 May 1989 261(17) pp2505-11
An analysis of US Food and Drug Administration data audits carried out between 1977 and 1988 which shows serious deficiencies in 12% of the pre-1985 audits, declining to 7% after that date when new control procedures were developed. Concludes that the data audit programme has been successful in reducing the frequency of detected misconduct, but that further measures could be taken including the penalisation of drug manufacturers for misconduct. For more on the potential of data audit as a tool in reducing the incidence of misconduct
See also: [Data audit] (Accountability in Research, 1990 1(2) Complete issue)
Data audit by a regulatory agency: its effect and implications for others, by M F Shapiro (Accountability in Research, 1992 2(3) pp219-29, 11 references)
Scientific data audit: a key management tool, by J L Glick (Accountability in Research, 1992 2(3) pp153-68)
Data audits in investigational drug trials and their implications for detection of misconduct in science, by M F Shapiro (In: Fraud and misconduct in medical research, edited by S Lock and F Wells. BMJ Publishing: London, 1993 pp128-41, 10 references)

(63)
BALTIMORE throws in the towel
Hamilton, D P and Baltimore, D
Science, 10 May 1991 252(5007) pp768-70
The text of David Baltimore's 'mea culpa' statement exonerating Margot O'Toole, the whistleblower in the case of immunologist Thereza Imanishi-Kari who published an allegedly fraudulent paper in the journal *Cell*, co-authored by Nobel laureate David Baltimore. This case, which has still not been finally settled, has been covered exhaustively by the scientific press (particularly *Science* and *Nature*) and by more specialist journals. For some of the more extensive analysis, including a book by journalist Judy Sarasohn
See also: Questions of scientific responsibility: the Baltimore case, by S Lang (Ethics and Behavior, 1993 3(1) pp3-72, numerous references)
On Margot O'Toole and the Baltimore case: a personal note on the evolution of my involvement, by J T Edsall (Ethics and Behavior, 1994 4(3) pp239-47, 13 references)
Science on trial: the whistle blower, the accused, and the Nobel laureate, by J Sarasohn (St Martin's Press; New York, 1993. 294pp)

(64)
MISCONDUCT and fraud in research: social and legislative issues symposium of the Society of University Surgeons
Mavroudis, C and others
Surgery, Jul 1991 110(1) pp1-7, 16 references
Summarises the results of a questionnaire survey of active members of the Society in 1989: 204 (82%) returned responses. Seven questions dealt with definitions of fraud, and eight with the perception or recognition of fraud. Forty per cent were aware of at least one incident of fraud that had been openly investigated in their institutions, and 43% were aware of at least one 'quiet' inquiry. Nearly 30% had directly refuted data published

by a colleague, and 15% strongly suspected that incidents of fraud had occurred and not been investigated by their institutions. Also includes responses on the correction and reduction of fraud, which are overwhelmingly in favour of strong academic penalties.

(65)
EXPOSURE: the whistleblower, the nemesis, and the press
In: Stealing into print: fraud, plagiarism, and misconduct in scientific publishing, by M C
    LaFollette
    University of California Press: Berkeley, CA, 1992 pp137-55
Discusses the nature of whistleblowing by insiders or nemesis figures such as Walter W Stewart and Ned Feder who have become highly controversial figures in the American scientific community. Stresses the costs which whistleblowers may have to pay using the case of Margot O'Toole in the so-called Baltimore affair as an example. Further comment on Stewart and Feder's long battle to publish their article on John Darsee's co-authors is given in Chapter 1 (pp8-13). For comment on the 1995 official reprimand issued by the National Institutes of Health for breaching a 1993 order to refrain from investigating misconduct cases at government expense, and for its subsequent withdrawal
See also: On their own: Stewart and Feder persist with misconduct inquiries, by
F Hoke (Scientist, 6 Feb 1995 9(3) pp3-4)
Feder, Stewart rapped for letter on NIH stationery (Science and Government Report, 1
Mar 1995 25(4) pp3-4)
NIH's reprimanded pair receive a de-reprimand (Science and Government Report,
15 Apr 1995 25(7) pp4-5)

(66)
FALSE prophets: fraud and error in science and medicine: new edition
A Kohn
Blackwell: Oxford, 1992. 248pp
A set of case studies, historical and modern, of fraudulent and aberrant research in the natural sciences, medicine, psychology and archaeology. Originally published in 1986.

(67)
SCIENTIFIC ethics and responsibility: AAAS member opinion poll: summary report of key findings
American Association for the Advancement of Science, Office of Membership and Circulation, 1333 H Street NW, Washington, DC 20005, Mar 1992. Unpaged
Presents data and opinions from a survey of 469 AAAS members, 27% of whom claim to have witnessed or encountered suspected fraudulent behaviour in the previous ten years. Covers a wide range of issues dealing with the detection, prevention, investigation and disciplining of such behaviour. For comment and summary
See also: In the trenches: doubts about scientific integrity, by D P Hamilton (Science, 27 Mar 1992 255(5052) p1636)
The scientific community perspective on research integrity, by A H Teich
(Accountability in Research, 1993 3(2/3) pp117-22, 3 references)

(68)
REFLECTIONS of a whistleblower
Rossiter, E J R
Nature, 11 Jun 1992 357(6378) pp434-36
A personal account from the man who exposed a case of scientific misconduct in Australia by scientist Michael Briggs.

(69)
BETRAYERS of the truth: fraud and deceit in science: new edition
Broad, W and Wade, N
Simon and Schuster: New York, 1993. 256pp
A much-quoted and controversial study which covers many historical cases of deception as well as more modern ones reported in the journals *Science* and *New Scientist*. For more recent comment from Broad and Wade
See also: Fraud and the structure of science, by W Broad and N Wade (In: Ethical issues in scientific research: an anthology, edited by E Erwin and others. Garland Publishing: London, 1994 pp69-89)

(70)
MISCONDUCT in medical research
Hals, A and Jacobsen, G
Tidsskrift for den Norske Laegeforening, 1993 113(25) pp3149-52 (In Norwegian)
Presents the results of a survey of research project administrators whose study protocols were assessed by the ethical committee for biomedical research in Health Region 4 in central Norway. The survey, which was carried out between 1986 and 1992, focuses on medical ethics and the scientists' views of the committee, but also included a request for comment on seven statements about scientific fraud and misconduct.

(71)
ON being a whistleblower: the Needleman case
Ernhart, C B and others
Ethics and Behavior, 1993 3(1) pp73-93, 32 references
The whistleblowers in the Needleman case, which involved influential research findings on the effects of low level exposure to lead in children, discuss their role. Their actions were based on the premise that members of the scientific community have an overriding obligation to promote integrity in research. In this particular case the fact that Needleman's work has had a considerable impact on public policy is especially influential. For further comment, including a riposte from Herbert Needleman
See also: Reply to Ernhart, Scarr, and Geneson, by H L Needleman (Ethics and Behavior, 1993 3(1) pp95-101, 13 references)
Of whistleblowers, investigators, and judges, by S Scarr and C B Ernhart (Ethics and Behavior, 1993 3(2) pp199-206, 21 references)
Protection of the public interest, allegations of misconduct and the Needleman case, by E K Silbergeld (American Journal of Public Health, Feb 1995 85(2) pp165-66, 6 references)

(72)
RESEARCH misconduct: a resumé of recent events
Lock, S
In: Fraud and misconduct in medical research, edited by S Lock and F Wells
    BMJ Publishing: London, 1993 pp5-24
Gives details of known or suspected scientific fraud gleaned from the biomedical literature covering the period since the early 1970s. Includes cases from Australia, the UK, the USA and other countries. Stephen Lock and Frank Wells' book is to be reissued in updated form in 1995. For their contributions to a mini-symposium on scientific misconduct in medical research
See also: Management of research misconduct – in practice, by F O Wells (Journal of Internal Medicine, Feb 1994 235(2) pp115-122)

Research misconduct: a brief history and a comparison, by S Lock (Journal of Internal Medicine, Feb 1994 235(2) pp123-28)

(73)
WHISTLEBLOWING: a very unpleasant avocation
Sprague, R L

Ethics and Behavior, 1993 3(1) pp103-33, 34 references

A first person account of the events surrounding the investigation and prosecution of Stephen E Breuning for scientific fraud. His case involved the falsification of data on the impact of the withdrawal of certain tranquillising drugs from the treatment of severely mentally handicapped children. Some US states changed their treatment protocols as a result of Breuning's fraud. Looks in detail at the adverse consequences for the whistleblower.

(74)
A SUCCESSFUL system of scientific data audits for clinical trials
Weiss, R B and others

Journal of the American Medical Association, 28 Jul 1993 270(4) pp459-64, 17 references

Presents the results of data audits carried out on members of the Cancer and Leukemia Group B which show a very low incidence of impropriety in clinical trials (only two instances over an eleven year period, both before 1984). Audits have, however, had a measurable impact on the administrative efficiency of units in respect of consent forms, institutional review board approval and ancillary data submission. (It is, however, interesting to note that one of the institutions whose data were passed by the CALGB has subsequently been accused of passing false data to the National Surgical Adjuvant Breast and Bowel Project. Clearly data audits do not always provide unambiguous evidence. For a letter which comments on this issue

See also: Audit of Cancer and Leukemia Group B data, by W C Wood (New England Journal of Medicine, 28 Jul 1994 331(4) p279)

(75)
ETHICAL problems in academic research
Swazey, J P and others

American Scientist, Nov/Dec 1993 81(6) pp542-53, 12 references

Presents the results of a survey of 2,000 doctoral students and 2,000 faculty members from 99 of the largest US graduate departments in chemistry, civil engineering, microbiology and sociology. The data suggest that though misconduct (restricted to data falsification and plagiarism) is not rampant, it is by no means rare. Between 6 and 9% of students and faculty reported direct knowledge of falsification or plagiarism by faculty members; and nearly 30% of faculty members claim to have observed student plagiarism. Other forms of ethically questionable behaviour may be much more common. These include exploitation, discrimination, sexual harassment (especially in sociology departments), the misuse of research funds, and the failure to comply with rules on the ethical conduct of research. For brief summaries and comment

See also: Survey tracks misconduct to an extent, by C Anderson (Science, 19 Nov 1993 262(5137) pp1203-04)

Survey finds researchers often encounter scientific misconduct, by P S Zurer (Chemical and Engineering News, 22 Nov 1993 71(47) pp24-25)

(76)
SCIENTIFIC misconduct: not just someone else's problem
L Rothenberg
Trends in Biotechnology, Feb 1994 12(2) pp35-39, 7 references
A brief review of developments in responses to scientific misconduct in the USA is followed by a table of closed cases of research misconduct published by the Office of Research Integrity in 1993. For each case, includes brief details of location, nature of misconduct (plagiarism, fabrication etc), details of conduct, and sanctions imposed. Individuals are identified only by their initials. Details of cases completed in 1994 are given in the ORI's second annual report (Ref. 184, Ch. 3).

(77)
ETHICAL challenges to risk scientists: an exploratory analysis of survey data
Greenberg, M and Goldberg, L
Science, Technology and Human Values, Spring 1994 19(2) pp223-41, 31 references
Surveys of nearly 1,500 members of three professional US societies undertaking risk analysis are presented. A third of respondents had observed biased research design, 20% had witnessed plagiarism, and 10% data falsification.

(78)
SCIENTIFIC misconduct in environmental science and toxicology
Nigg, H N and Radulescu, G
Journal of the American Medical Association, 13 Jul 1994 272(2) pp168-70, 17 references
Argues that misconduct can occur easily in environmental science, and describes four cases, one discovered by an editor and the other three reported by other authors. Finds that scientific misconduct may occur undetected across phyla, genera and species; that distance from the publishing source makes detection more difficult; that editors and reviewers are not organised to take action against misconduct; that plagiarised authors are likely to report the offence if detected; and that there is only a small risk of censure from any source for environmental scientists engaging in deceptive behaviour.

2.2 Why scientists may deceive

2.2(a) Personality factors

Although undue emphasis may have been placed on personality disorders as an explanation for scientific deception, they cannot be ignored, especially in cases of gross misconduct or those involving exceptionally talented individuals. It is, for example, difficult to understand why the brilliant young cardiologist, John Darsee, cheated systematically throughout his entire career when his talent was certainly great enough to have taken him to the top of his profession by the normal route (Ref. 83). Equally, it is hard to reconcile Louis Pasteur's unquestioned status as a great man of science with evidence that he regularly misrepresented his work in order to marginalise opponents and gain public confidence, funding and prestige (Ref. 88).

The fact is, that however brilliant, every scientist is also a human being with commonplace human desires to be recognised, rewarded and remembered. Indeed, it may be the strength of those desires which distinguishes the great scientist from the everyday one. 'Greed for applause' or the determined pursuit of a favoured hypothesis which the researcher *knows* intuitively is right can, sometimes, lead predisposed individuals to create or manipulate the 'truth' rather than discover it. Such deliberate deception is not the same as honest error or unwitting self-deception, neither of which are uncommon in science, and perpetrators will often seek to avoid personal responsibility if challenged. They may claim mental exhaustion, intolerable pressures of work, moral justification (the end justifies the means) or other reasons for their conduct, but a simple admission of wrong-doing and acceptance of responsibility for it are rare.

Many of the more notorious cases of misconduct described in *Science under siege* (Ref. 121), *Betrayers of the truth* (Ref. 69), *False prophets* (Ref. 66), *Impure science* (Ref. 126) and other sources have been ascribed to personality disorders. For example, Dr William McBride's attempts to show that Debendox, like Thalidomide, was responsible for birth defects have been attributed to (or excused by) his unshakeable belief in the dangers of the drug which led him to falsify data 'in the long term interests of humanity'. However, some might suspect that a desire to maintain his status as a millionaire 'hero' of science also played a part (Ref. 86). The perverted desire for hero status, and the money that goes with it, is also evident in some historic frauds including those allegedly perpetrated by archaeologist Heinrich Schliemann in the last century (Ref. 89).

The cold fusion saga, in contrast, may be more characteristic of self-deception in the pursuit of a holy grail of science, a suspension of critical faculties which, in this case, extended well beyond the researchers themselves to the scientific community at large which is described by Gary Taubes as abandoning traditional scientific caution and method in its eagerness to confirm the results of Pons and Fleischmann's experiments (Ref. 87). Charles Dawson's 'discovery' of Piltdown Man (Ref. 79) and Sir Cyril Burt's fabrication of data on IQ have also been described as products of self-deception, the latter brought on by Burt's 'secrecy, suspicion of rivals, egocentricity, compulsive motivation and hypochondria'. Other commentators are equally sure that Burt knew exactly what he was doing or, conversely, that he was unjustly accused by jealous colleagues and juniors (Ref. 82).

Some of the best known cases of deception may tell the scientific community as much about its own collective personality characteristics as those of the individuals concerned – not only its susceptibility to charisma and power which can sometimes blind it to the unacceptable activities of 'great' or outstandingly talented individuals, but its willingness to collude with some deceivers in using mental aberration as an excuse for behaviour which in any other walk of life would be deemed unambiguously criminal. For example, in the case of William Summerlin, who falsified skin graft evidence on a mouse because of the allegedly intolerable pressures he was under, the immediate response of his superiors was to offer him a year's paid sick leave (Ref. 80).

That a very small minority of scientists may be mentally ill, emotionally disturbed or criminally deviant is not in doubt – the scientific community is no more immune from these problems than any other group of people. However, to attribute all breaches of ethical norms to personal inadequacies ignores the fact that there are many other, external influences on scientists which may lead them into deceptive behaviour: perhaps not on the grand scale, but still to a degree which may be damaging. Equally important, the scientific establishment, and those public and private organisations with an interest in science, cannot escape responsibility for these influences which are an integral part of the way in which science is organised, funded and managed.

(79)
THE PILTDOWN forgery
Weiner, J S
Oxford University Press, 1955. 214pp (Republished in 1991 by Dover Press: New York, and Constable Press: London)
For more on this famous case of scientific fraud
See also: The Piltdown inquest, by C Blinderman (Prometheus: Buffalo, 1986. 261pp)
Piltdown: a scientific forgery, by F Spencer (Oxford University Press, 1990. 232pp)
The Piltdown papers, by F Spencer (Natural History Museum: London, 1990. 282pp)

(80)
THE PATCHWORK mouse
Hixson, J
Anchor Press/Doubleday: Garden City, NY, 1976. 228pp
Deals with the William Summerlin affair which is credited with stimulating the current wave of interest in scientific fraud and misconduct in the USA. He claimed to have overcome the rejection problems inherent in transplantation during research in which he transplanted skin grafts between black and white animals of different genetic strains. It transpired that he had artificially darkened black skin grafts on a white animal using a felt tipped pen. He was given sick leave, and ultimately dismissed. The Summerlin case is covered by most of the major analyses of scientific deception listed in this review.

(81)
A VIEW of misconduct in science
Racker, E
Nature, 11 May 1989 339(6220) pp91-93
An eminent biochemist argues, on the basis of a case in his own laboratory, that fraud committed by talented professionals arises from mental unbalance. Each case must be handled individually, and pursued in the courts if warranted. The case involved a graduate student, Mark Spector, who fabricated a whole series of experiments in the cancer field. For more on this case
See also: Science's faulty fraud detectors, by W J Broad and N Wade (Psychology Today, Nov 1982 16(11) pp51-54,57)

(82)
SCIENCE, ideology and the media: the Cyril Burt scandal
Fletcher, R
Transaction Publishers: New Brunswick, NJ, 1991. 419pp, bibliography pp405-11
There is a very large volume of publications on the Burt case, to which this analysis gives some access. For later comment on the possibility that Burt was the victim of malicious accusation
See also: Cyril Burt: fraud or framed? edited by N J Mackintosh (Oxford University Press, Jul 1995. 156pp)

(83)
CARDIOLOGY: the John Darsee experience
Braunwald, E
In: Research fraud in the behavioural and biomedical sciences, edited by D J Miller and
    M Hersen
    Wiley: Chichester, 1992 pp55-79, 4 references
A useful resumé of the complex Darsee case by the professor in charge of him at Harvard Medical School.

(84)
CHARACTER and the ethical conduct of research
Pellegrino, E D
Accountability in Research, 1992 2(1) pp1-11, 34 notes and references
Looks at the nature of virtue ethics, both in general terms and in research, noting that the latter includes a commitment to truth and the expansion of human welfare. Fraud occurs when self-interest replaces truth as the ordering principle of science, an outcome which is increasingly likely given the modern ordering of science as an 'industrial activity'. Greater attention needs to be paid to strengthening those aspects of a scientist's character which are conducive to ethical conduct, initially by improvements in the teaching of scientific ethics.

(85)
PERSONALITY factors in scientific fraud and misconduct
Miller, D J
In: Research fraud in the behavioural and biomedical sciences, edited by D J Miller and M Hersen
    Wiley: Chichester, 1992 pp 125-39, 29 references
Looks at the kinds of personality traits which may make certain researchers more vulnerable to committing fraud or deception. Distinguishes between honest (but erroneous) assumptions, self-deception, and the conscious or deliberate intention to mislead, and looks at the kinds of explanations or justifications used by those whose fraudulent behaviour is discovered.

(86)
SCIENTIFIC fraud: the McBride case
Humphrey, G F
Medicine, Science and the Law, Jul 1992 32(3) pp199-203, 8 references
An analysis of William McBride's attempts to prove that Debendox, like Thalidomide, caused birth defects. He was subsequently removed from the medical register, a decision which he challenged unsuccessfully in the courts. For subsequent comment on McBride's fate, and for his later autiobiography in which he continues to assert his innocence
See also: William McBride's penalty, by M Ragg (Lancet, 7 Aug 1993 342(8867) pp361-62)
Killing the messenger, by W McBride (Eldorado: Cremona, New South Wales, 1994. 287pp)

(87)
BAD science: the short life and hard times of cold fusion
Taubes, G
Random House: New York, 1993. 503pp
For more on this case, including the argument (by Mallove) that the scientific community has been over-hasty in condemning a promising field of inquiry
See also: Fire from ice: searching for truth beyond the cold fusion furore, by E F Mallove (Wiley: New York, 1991. 334pp)
Too hot to handle: the race for cold fusion, by F E Close (Penguin: Harmondsworth, 1992. 388pp)
Cold fusion: the scientific fiasco of the century: revised edition, by J R Huizenga (University of Rochester Press: Rochester, NJ, 1993. 318pp)

(88)
THE PRIVATE science of Louis Pasteur
Geison, G
Princeton University Press, 1995. 411pp
A biography of Pasteur based on access to many of his laboratory notebooks. These reveal that Pasteur failed to acknowledge that he borrowed the technique for making a vaccine against anthrax from a competitor, that he experimented on humans without consent, and sometimes misrepresented his work in order to attract funding and scientific prestige.

(89)
SCHLIEMANN of Troy: treasure and deceit
Traill, D A
John Murray: London, 1995. 365pp
A study based on many years' study of Schliemann's activities in Troy and Mycenae which suggests that some of his publications and artefacts were fraudulent. Schliemann, it is argued, was a liar who imported the ethics of the marketplace into scientific inquiry for personal and financial gain. Traill's study has been heavily reviewed in the broadsheet newspaper press and other publications, suggesting considerable interest in the issue of scientific deception.

2.2(b) The pressure to publish

Ultimately, of course, it is the individual's personality that determines how he or she will behave. However, it would be foolish to deny that human conduct is also shaped by the circumstances in which one lives and works. The ethical principles of science are, as already discussed, fluid and open to interpretation even at the most 'criminal' end of the deception spectrum, and the response of the individual is likely to be heavily conditioned by circumstance. It is the contention of many who are concerned at the apparent increase in deceptive behaviour that the scientist's traditional adherence to high standards of conduct is being put under intolerable pressure by what Beth Savan calls 'the academic hustle' (Ref. 97).

All aspiring academic scientists know that, in order to make their mark, they must be prolific both in research and publication. Research productivity is closely linked to salary, promotion, the achievement of tenure and the award of research funding, and the key mechanism through which the links are made is the scientific publishing system. A scientist's merit is measured by the number and quality of the papers he or she has published, the latter often judged in terms of the degree to which they are cited by others. Since publication is clearly necessary as a means of disseminating and verifying new scientific knowledge, this system would appear to be an eminently sensible one.

However, the inexorable pressure to publish is now increasingly recognised as an evil (albeit one which tends to be reflected in wry jokes rather than protests) in which the research paper has become an end rather than a means (Ref. 90). It is arguable that scientists no longer publish predominantly to disseminate new knowledge – this function is increasingly carried out by informal means, either electronically or through face-to-face contact at conferences – but to boost their curriculum vitae or the research ratings of their departments. As more and more papers appear, the competition for inclusion in the most prestigious journals becomes ever more intense, fuelling yet more publishing because a key criterion used by peer reviewers is likely to be an author's previous publication record.

The system, which was already threatening to become unsustainable as a result of its own internal dynamics, has been tipped further over the edge in recent years by the adoption in some countries (including the UK) of quantitative research assessment indicators, and their use in the allocation of public research funding. These include publications data and have been a further stimulus both to the quantity of publishing and its distortion as a dissemination medium.

Deception or expediency?

The kinds of behaviour which result from this subversion of the publication system to ends for which it was never designed are often described by scientists as expedient rather than deceptive, although their impact may still be damaging. They include 'salami publishing', or the breaking down of research findings to the 'least publishable unit' in order to create as many papers as possible, and its mirror image, 'imalas publishing', which involves the reissue of previously published material with slight additions; the multiple publication of the same findings in slightly different versions for different journals (a tactic which is only too obvious to those who work in the information profession); and the inclusion as authors of people with minimal practical involvement in the research (Ref. 115).

Multiple authorship, which, as already noted, is increasing to the point of absurdity in some cases, is not necessarily a manipulative tactic designed to deceive. Indeed, the main impetus is probably provided by the growth of very large scale collaborative research programmes, particularly in the particle physics and biomedical fields. However, where it involves honorary authors, it may certainly shade into deception in the sense that it presents an inaccurate picture of responsibility for particular pieces of research, may artificially inflate the reputations of some individuals, and prevent close scrutiny of the activities of others. It can also lay unwitting authors open to contamination by association with more serious forms of misconduct as Stewart and Feder's analysis of papers published by John Darsee suggests (Ref. 95).

The enormous power exercised by publications ratings in the scientific world may, however, produce behaviour which is quite clearly deceptive, encapsulated in the title of Marcel LaFollette's analysis of the scientific publishing system, *Stealing into print* (Ref. 109). There may, for example, be a greater temptation to plagiarise the work of others in order to boost a personal publications record, or to give unwarranted prominence to one's own work, or that of certain colleagues, in citations. Equally, there may be a temptation to underplay the contribution made by competitors or intellectual predecessors. Bibliometricians, who are practised in the arcane arts of analysing publications data, claim that such manipulative behaviour is both rare and easily detected, but many research scientists would disagree.

One area of deception which may be particularly difficult to detect is discussed by the North American editor of the *British Medical Journal*, Richard Horton, in a recent article on the rhetoric of research (Ref. 119). While journal editors and grant awarding bodies may take considerable pains over scientific and statistical peer review, insufficient attention is paid to the qualitative aspects of scientific communication – 'the manipulation of language to convince the reader of the likely truth of a result'. Authors do not seek to present the reader with options in their text which rather 'describes a specific path, carefully carved by the authors, through a complex undergrowth of competing arguments'. A careful peer reviewer needs to understand the nature of this path and the way it is constructed in linguistic terms, in order to arrive at an objective evaluation. Though Horton's thesis is challenged in the same issue of the *BMJ* by a medical writer who argues that linguistic spin should be celebrated rather than condemned, it does seem one worth considering given the acknowledged pressure on researchers to report positive results (Ref. 112).

Retraction of fradulent material

The explosion in scientific publishing may not only tempt researchers into deceptive or manipulative behaviour; it may also make the detection of serious misconduct and the eradication of its effects more difficult. The journal peer review system has been placed under intense pressure as a result of the avalanche of research manuscripts, and is increasingly accused of failing in its primary duty. In the words of journal editor Drummond Rennie, writing in the *Journal of the American Medical Association* in 1986: 'There seems to be no study too fragmented, no hypothesis too trivial, no literature citation too biased or too egotistical, no design too warped, no methodology too bungled, no presentation of results too inaccurate, too obscure, and too contradictory, no analysis too self-serving, no argument too circular, no conclusions too trifling or too unjustified, and no grammar and syntax too offensive for a paper to end up in print' (Ref. 99).

If Rennie is correct, it is highly likely that multiple publication of the same material, plagiarism and data falsification or manipulation will pass unnoticed on occasion. Moreover, it may be difficult to root out known fraudulent literature once it has been published. Some evidence, for example in connection with the work of Robert Slutsky, suggests that the scientific community tends to shun work once it has been publicly stated to be fraudulent (Ref. 115). However, other analyses such as those by Mark Pfeifer and Gwendolyn Snodgrass, and Carol Kochan and John Budd, indicate that large numbers of fraudulent articles continue to be cited after retraction (Refs. 102, 110). This is not only because the articles continue to exist in the primary literature after formal retractions have been published. The problem is greatly magnified by the secondary sources of scientific literature – the abstracting and indexing services, computerised and hard copy – which scientists use for literature searching.

The producers of such services have no agreed policy on how or when to respond to fraudulent material. *Chemical Abstracts* took the decision, when it was still primarily a print-based service, to expunge such articles from its database altogether, but other producers take a quite different approach. There is a strong tradition among information professionals that they have no business acting as censors, and that their role should be as neutral purveyors and disseminators of information. In the context of secondary sources, this means that indexing and abstracting services should record the progress of an article, warts and all, rather than 'rewrite the history of science by eliminating references to discredited articles'.

The problem with this approach is the practical difficulties involved in linking such articles to subsequent retractions, including the basic question of what indexing term should be used to indicate a discredited piece of work. Some services such as MEDLINE have made considerable progress in ensuring that retrievals of fraudulent articles automatically trigger details of retractions, but this is not the case with all databases and not even MEDLINE differentiates between fraud and honest error (Ref. 118). Users must develop sophisticated search skills, and remain on their guard, to ensure that they gain the whole story.

The editors of scientific journals, and the producers of secondary services, clearly have an important role to play in the detection and remedying of deception, but they cannot be more than a second line of defence behind the scientific community itself. Indeed, it has been argued that the criticism of journals, and pressures on editors to act as 'a Maginot line against unethical behaviour', are partly a response to the failure of universities to police their researchers adequately. Considerable progress has been made by the scientific publishing community, for example the Council of Biology Editors and the International Committee of Medical Journal Editors (the 'Vancouver Group'), in exploring the issues and developing standards and protocols (Refs. 100, 106, 114). However, the practical difficulties facing editors remain immense.

Moreover, the rapid advance of technology, including the development of electronic journals, raises a whole new set of problems. Although some commentators such as Davenport and Cronin see the advent of new technologies as a means of transforming the practice and culture of science for the better, others are not so sure (Ref. 105). Marcel LaFollette, herself once editor of *Science, Technology and Human Values*, argues that technical change may make life easier for the honest researcher but it also offers unparalleled new opportunities for the deceiver to work undetected. In 1983 the editor of the *New England Journal of Medicine* argued that there is no practical alternative to the 'presumption of honesty in research, because it would be impossible to verify every primary datum and every descriptive statement in a research report' (Ref. 91). Twelve years on, the explosion of scientific publishing, both hard copy and electronic, is such that trust in the ethical conduct of scientists must still remain the mainspring of editorial practice.

(90)
WINNING the games scientists play
Sindermann, C J
Plenum Press: New York, 1982. 290pp
A light-hearted, rather cynical, account by a marine biologist who looks, among other things, at the manipulation of the scientific publishing system by scientists to boost their own status.

(91)
LESSONS from the Darsee affair
Relman, A S
New England Journal of Medicine, 9 Jun 1983 308(23) pp1415-17
Takes the view that, though improvements in the scientific publishing system could and should be made, the practical difficulties of checking every claim made by an author are insurmountable. The traditional system based on trust in the scientist's integrity and review by peers is still the best, though not infallible. For more from Arnold Relman
See also: How good is peer review? by A S Relman and M Angell (New England Journal of Medicine, 21 Sep 1989 321(12) pp827-29, 10 references)
Publishing biomedical research: roles and responsibilities, by A S Relman (Hastings Center Report, May/Jun 1990 20(3) pp23-27, 5 references)

(92)
[PEER review]
Science, Technology and Human Values, Summer 1985 10(3) Complete issue
A special issue on peer review in both the assessment of research proposals and in
scientific publishing. For more on peer review from this period
See also: Refereeing and peer review: Part 1 – opinion and conjecture on the
effectiveness of refereeing, by E Garfield (Current Contents, 4 Aug 1986 (31) pp3-11)
Refereeing and peer review: Part 2 – the research on refereeing and alternatives to the
present system, by E Garfield (Current Contents, 11 Aug 1986 (32) pp3-12)
Refereeing and peer review: Part 3 – how the peer review of research-grant proposals
works, and what scientists say about it, by E Garfield (Current Contents, 26 Jan 1987 (4)
pp3-8)
Refereeing and peer review: Part 4 – research on the peer review of grant proposals and
suggestions for improvement, by E Garfield (Current Contents, Feb 1987 (5) pp3-9)

(93)
FRAUD, irresponsible authorship and their causes
Annals of Internal Medicine, Feb 1986 104(2) pp252-62, 31 references
A set of five papers by R G Petersdorf, P K Woolf, E J Huth, J C Bailar and M Angell
dealing with subjects such as the pathogenesis of fraud in medical science, the impact of
the pressure to publish, and irresponsible authorship. Some were subsequently
republished in the following compilation
See also: The ethical dimensions of the biological sciences, edited by R E Bulger and
others (Cambridge University Press, 1993. 305pp)

(94)
BELIEVING what you read: responsibilities of medical authors and editors
Schiedermayer, D L and Siegler, M
Archives of Internal Medicine, Oct 1986 146(10) pp2043-44, 15 references
Notes the increasing rate at which authors and co-authors of scholarly medical papers are
withdrawing them because of fraud or scientific inaccuracy. Argues that there is a need
for a reappraisal of the ethical responsibilities of authors, editors and reviewers to ensure
higher standards.

(95)
THE INTEGRITY of the scientific literature
Stewart, W W and Feder, N
Nature, 15 Jan 1987 325(6101) pp207-14
Stewart and Feder's controversial paper published after a wait of four years during which
they were threatened with libel actions by co-authors of 18 fraudulent papers published
by cardiologist John Darsee. The 13 listed 'honorary' authors had little direct
involvement with the research, and all of the papers included significant errors and
discrepancies which had escaped the notice of co-authors, journal peer reviewers and
editors. For a response from Eugene Braunwald, Darsee's Professor at Harvard Medical
School, on the alleged lapses of co-authors
See also: On analysing scientific fraud, by E Braunwald (Nature, 15 Jan 1987 325(6101)
pp215-16)

(96)
ENSURING integrity in biomedical publication
Woolf, P K
Journal of the American Medical Association, 18 Dec 1987 258(23) pp3424-27,
22 references
Discusses the role of the editors of scientific journals in ensuring the high quality and integrity of the research they publish. Urges action in areas such as defining and enforcing standards of responsible authorship, establishing policies for retaining data for scrutiny, for publishing retractions, and enforcing peer review.

(97)
GETTING into print
In: Science under siege: the myth of objectivity in scientific research, by B Savan
   CBC Enterprises: Montreal, 1988 pp109-27, 64 notes and references
Identifies the 'unsavoury practices' which arise from the desperate need to publish combined with the increasing difficulty in getting manuscripts accepted by the most prestigious journals. Looks at problems with the peer review system and suggests new ways of ensuring that fraudulent or poor quality work is detected.

(98)
RESPONSIBILITY of the learned journal
Dusseau, J L
Perspectives in Biology and Medicine, Spring 1989 32(3) pp344-48, 10 references

(99)
EDITORS and auditors
Rennie, D
Journal of the American Medical Association, 5 May 1989 261(17) pp2543-45,
24 references
Puts forward a controversial proposal for the introduction of data audits as a check on fraudulent publication. For more comment by Drummond Rennie, including his 1986 *JAMA* editorial with its trenchant criticism of the peer review system
See also: Guarding the guardians: a conference on editorial peer review, by D Rennie (Journal of the American Medical Association, 7 Nov 1986 256(27) pp2391-92)
Accountability, audit and reverence for the publication process, by D Rennie (Journal of the American Medical Association, 28 Jul 1993 270(4) pp495-96, 16 references)

(100)
ETHICS and policy in scientific publication
Council of Biology Editors, Editorial Policy Committee
Council of Biology Editors: Bethesda, MD, 1990. 290pp, references
A two part work. Part 1 presents the results of opinion surveys carried out in relation to 19 ethical 'scenarios' which might face a scientific editor or publisher. They include issues such as allegations of data falsification, bias against negative results, disputes over authorship and confidentiality of reviews. Part 2 presents the proceedings of a conference held at the National Academy of Sciences in October 1988. The papers and discussion are grouped into sections covering the control of research data; allegations of fraud; responsible authorship; the misrepresentation of honest data; repetitive publication; legal problems in scientific reporting; and peer review.

(101)
MINIMIZING the three stages of publication bias
Chalmers, T C and others
Journal of the American Medical Association, 9 Mar 1990 263(10) pp1392-95,
25 references

The three stages are pre-publication bias caused by sloppy or fraudulent research practices; publication bias by editors or reviewers; and post-publication bias in the interpretation, review and meta-analysis of published clinical work. Bias can be minimised by insisting on high quality research practices and thorough literature reviews; the elimination of the double standard concerning peer review and informed consent; publishing legitimate clinical trials regardless of outcome; requiring peer reviewers to acknowledge possible conflicts of interest; replacing ordinary review articles by meta-analyses; and requiring the authors of reviews to acknowledge possible conflicts of interest. This article, and the two which follow, are contributions to the First International Congress on Editorial Peer Review in Biomedical Publication. An article from the report of the Second International Congress is listed below at Ref. 114.

(102)
THE CONTINUED use of retracted, invalid scientific literature
Pfeifer, M P and Snodgrass, G L
Journal of the American Medical Association, 9 Mar 1990 263(10) pp1420-23,
20 references

Presents the results of a citation analysis of 82 articles formally retracted from the literature because of fraud or error. The articles were cited 733 times after retraction, with a small number of citations referring to the retraction as well as the original article. Concludes that articles citing invalid work are 'abundant and ubiquitous', and identifies reasons why such work is not being effectively purged from the literature. For more on this issue
See also: Correcting the literature following fraudulent publication, by P J Friedman (Journal of the American Medical Association, 9 Mar 1990, 263(10) pp1416-19)

(103)
THE IMPACT of fraudulent research on the scientific literature: the Stephen E Breuning case
Garfield, E and Welljams-Dorof, A
Journal of the American Medical Association, 9 Mar 1990 263(10) pp1424-26
Examines the research impact of research fraud using citation analysis of 20 Breuning publications which received 200 citations, 40% by Breuning himself or his co-authors. Citations by other scientists declined sharply after 1986 when the fraud was disclosed. It is also evident that the vast majority of non-self citations were either negative or neutral as far as the work of other scientists was concerned.

(104)
MECHANISMS for evaluating scientific information and the role of peer review
Abelson, P H
Journal of the American Society of Information Science, Apr 1990 41(3) pp216-22, 9 references

The editor of the journal *Science* discusses the role of peer review and the mechanisms for evaluating scientific manuscripts. Argues that the pressure to 'publish or perish' has had an adverse effect on scientific communication, and recommends a more realistic approach to the evaluation of research productivity. The Darsee and Slutsky cases are used to illustrate weaknesses of the current system, but it is maintained that fraud (as opposed to unintended error) remains uncommon in science. For a more recent analysis of the journal peer review system and its problems

See also: Guardians of science: fairness and reliability of peer-review systems, by H-D Daniel (VCH: Weinheim, 1993. 118pp)

(105)
HYPERTEXT and the conduct of science
Davenport, E and Cronin, B

Journal of Documentation, Sep 1990 46(3) pp175-92, 48 references

Argues that hypertext may transform the practice and culture of science by making texts available for comment and verification in ways which have hitherto been impossible. As such, it may stimulate creativity, enable the more effective challenge of scientific orthodoxy and reduce the incidence of scientific fraud. For later comment on the issue of electronic communication and its impacts on the process and integrity of research and the peer review system

See also: Changing patterns of communication among scientists in an era of 'telescience', by L A Lievrouw and K Carley (Technology in Society, 1990 12(4) pp457-77)

The impact of tele-networking on research, by R Johnston (Prometheus, Dec 1994 12(2) pp225-45)

Publish and be robbed, by A Lawrence (New Scientist, 18 Feb 1995 145(1965) pp32-37)

Storming the barricades, by R Matthews (New Scientist, 17 Jun 1995 146(1982) pp38-41)

(106)
STATEMENTS from the International Committee of Medical Journal Editors
International Committee of Medical Journal Editors

Journal of the American Medical Association, 22/29 May 1991 265(20) pp2697-98, 7 references

The ICMJE (the 'Vancouver Group') was set up in 1978 and its guidance is widely followed by journal editors. Statements approved in February 1991 are reprinted here on order of authorship, patients' right to anonymity, and what to do about competing manuscripts based on the same study. Four other statements on confidentiality, the role of the correspondence column, editorial freedom and the retraction of research findings are also given. Further ICMJE statements are given below at Ref. 114. For comment on the need for the International Committee to develop a policy on editorial, as well as author, abuses

See also: Is there a case for an International Medical Scientific Press Council, by D G Altman and others (Journal of the American Medical Association, 13 Jul 1994 272(2) pp166-67, 7 references)

(107)
FRAUD: the journal's role concerning fraudulent research
Sharp, D W

Investigative Radiology, Jun 1991 26(6) pp586-89, 25 references

A general review of growing concern about scientific misconduct, and the role of journals in responding to it, which argues that 'the clearest duty lies in the prompt and effective publication of a retraction'.

(108)
EDITORIAL processes, safeguards and remedies
Freedman, D X
In: Research fraud in the behavioral and biomedical sciences, edited by D J Miller and
M Hersen
Wiley: Chichester, 1992 pp182-203, 18 references
Discusses the response of the scientific publishing community to the detection and
remedying of fraud, suggesting that there may be a danger of over-reaction. Describes
the editorial and review process, and measures which can be used to correct the
literature. Includes comment on the Stephen Breuning case.

(109)
**STEALING into print: fraud, plagiarism and misconduct in scientific
publishing**
LaFollette, M C
University of California Press: Berkeley: CA, 1992. 293pp, extensive notes and
bibliography
A detailed study by a one-time editor of *Science, Technology and Human Values* which
begins by looking at reasons why deception may occur, and attempting to define
deceptive behaviour. Her analysis of the scientific publication system looks at its
organisation and economics, the nature of authorship, the roles of editors and referees,
the problems faced by whistleblowers, the investigation of suspected fraud, its
punishment and the correction of the literature. Includes reference to many well known
cases, and discusses the possible implications of the electronic publishing revolution.
LaFollette also includes discussion of the fictional treatment of scientific deception in
books such as the following:
See also: The cantor's dilemma, by C Djerassi (Doubleday: New York, 1989. 229pp)
A novelist's view of scientific fraud [review of Djerassi's book], by R J Levene (Law,
Medicine and Health Care, Winter 1990 18(4) pp422-23)

(110)
THE PERSISTENCE of fraud in the literature: the Darsee case
Kochan, C A and Budd, J M
Journal of the American Society for Information Science, Aug 1992 43(7) pp488-493,
28 references
Describes the background to the Darsee case, and presents the results of a citation
analysis of his papers. Despite the wide publicity given to the case, and the retraction of
some of papers, Darsee's work continues to be cited positively in the literature of
cardiology. There are implications both for the biomedical and information
communities.

(111)
FRAUD and the editor
Lock, S
In: Fraud and misconduct in medical research, edited by S Lock and F Wells
BMJ Publishing: London, 1993 pp158-72, 29 references
A former editor of the *British Medical Journal* discusses the editorial process and the checks
which might be instituted to minimise the chances of fraudulent publication.

(112)
PUBLICATION bias: the problem that won't go away
Dickersin, K and Min, Y-I
In: Doing more good than harm: the evaluation of health care interventions: conference
   proceedings, edited by K S Warren and F Mosteller
   Annals of the New York Academy of Sciences, 1993 vol 703 pp135-48, 25
   references + discussion
Reviews the evidence to suggest that clinical trials are more likely to be reported if they
show a statistically significant difference between treatments, using data from four studies
in the USA and UK. The results suggest a strong bias towards the publication of positive
results, for which investigators rather than referees or editors are responsible. A similar
bias is evident in the reporting of clinical trial results by the lay press. Looks at ways in
which the under-reporting of negative or neutral scientific results can be challenged,
arguing that bias needs to be eradicated in the interests of patient safety. If those
reviewing the effects of health care treatment do not have all the evidence, it is possible
they they may reach the wrong conclusions on efficacy and safety.

(113)

THE SCIENTIFIC, technical and medical information systems in the UK
Royal Society, 6 Carlton House Terrace, London SW1Y 5AG, The British Library, and
the Association of Learned and Professional Society Publishers, 1993. 218pp (British
Library Research and Development Report 6213)
A useful analysis of developing trends in the scientific publishing and information system
including the development of electronic journals.

(114)

UNIFORM requirements for manuscripts submitted to biomedical journals
International Committee of Medical Journal Editors
Journal of the American Medical Association, 5 May 1993 269(17) pp2282-86
A slightly revised edition of the 4th edition of the Committee's recommendations on the
preparation and submission of manuscripts. Includes comment on prior and duplicate
publication, noting that multiple publication of the same study is only justifiable in a
very few, strictly defined, circumstances. For ICMJE statements on other ethical aspects
of publication
See also: Conflict of interest, by International Committee of Medical Journal Editors
(Lancet, 20 Mar 1993 341(8847) pp742-43)
Statement by the International Committee of Medical Journal Editors on duplicate or
redundant publication (Journal of the American Medical Association, 24 Nov 1993
270(20) p2495)
Advertising in medical journals and the use of supplements, by International Committee
of Medical Journal Editors (British Medical Journal, 25 Jun 1994 308(6945) p1692)

(115)

**THE SCIENTIFIC community's response to evidence of fraudulent
publication: the Slutsky, Robert case**
Whitely, W P and others
Journal of the American Medical Association, 13 Jul 1994 272(2) pp170-73
A contribution to The Second International Congress on Peer Review in Biomedical
Publication. Twenty-five further papers are published in this issue of *JAMA*. Whitely's
analysis of citation data suggests that scientists do not, and probably cannot, identify
published articles that are fraudulent. However, when alerted to the presence of

fraudulent results, they reduce the number of citations of the tainted work. Interestingly, formal journal retractions proved less effective than general news reporting in purging fraudulent results from the literature. For more on the Slutsky case and the lessons it offers about the climate of deception

See also: Misrepresentation and responsibility in medical research, by R L Engler and others (New England Journal of Medicine, 26 Nov 1989 317(22) pp1383-89, 9 references + appendix of Slutsky's bibliography)

(116)
PUBLICATION ethics: one of many areas of scientific fraud
Riis, P
Acta Obstetrica et Gynecologica Scandinavica, Aug 1994 73(7) pp526-28
Focuses on four issues associated with publication ethics: the definition of authorship; salami (and imalas) publishing; clandestine multiple publication; and the handling of alleged and proven dishonesty by journal editors. For a more detailed exposition by Povl Riis who is a member of the Danish Committee on Scientific Dishonesty

See also: The ethics of medical publishing and the four principles, by M Nylenna and P Riis (In: Principles of health care ethics, edited by R Gillon. Wiley: Chichester, 1994 pp783-94)

(117)
PLAYING fair: science, ethics and scientific journals
Edwards, G and others
Addiction, Jan 1995 90(1) pp3-8, 39 references
Editorial comment on the issue of publication ethics, with particular reference to the field of addiction research. Seeks to define an editorial position for *Addiction* on the ethical relationship between a journal and the scientific community.

(118)
ERRATA, retraction, duplicate publication, and comment policy
National Library of Medicine, National Institutes of Health, Bethesda, MD 20894, Apr 1995. 4pp (National Library of Medicine Fact Sheet)
Explains the National Library of Medicine's policy and practice on linking retrievals of fraudulent articles, or those reflecting honest errors, to subsequent retractions.

(119)
THE RHETORIC of research
Horton, R
British Medical Journal, 15 Apr 1995 310(6985) pp985-87, 9 references
Argues that peer review mechanisms take insufficient account of the use of linguistic manipulation by authors in order to convince the reader of the validity of their arguments, and looks at ways in which 'linguistic spin' can be detected and accounted for. For a critical response from a medical writer who argues that spin is unlikely to turn the scientific head, and provides the spice which enlivens scientific writing

See also: Commentary: scientific heads are not turned by rhetoric, by T Greenhalgh [with a riposte from Richard Horton] (British Medical Journal, 15 Apr 1995 310(6985) pp987-88, 9 references)

2.2(c) The academic rat race

Many proven cases of scientific deception involve young or middle-ranking scientists who are believed to be under particularly strong pressure because they are at the lower end of the career ladder. They need to develop good ideas, and get them published ahead of the opposition, if they are to achieve the reputation necessary for academic advancement, greater job security and a higher salary. In the British context, these pressures may well be exacerbated by the widespread use of short-term contract working for researchers until they are well into their twenties or early thirties, a practice which has been condemned by many in the scientific establishment but has continued unabated in the face of financial pressures on the universities (Ref. 133). Between 1977/78 and 1993/94 the number of wholly university-funded research staff rose from 32,000 to 32,750; the equivalent figures for contract staff are 5,900 and 18,600, a 217% increase.

While it would be insulting to suggest that job insecurity and poor terms and conditions of employment are conducive of deceptive behaviour, they are not the ideal environment in which to foster high standards of conduct. In July 1995 the Royal Society, the research councils, the Committee of Vice Chancellors and Principals and the Office of Science and Technology issued a consultative document designed to bring the terms and conditions of contract researchers into line with those of tenured collagues of equivalent rank. The aim is to provide much better career management, training and support for contract staff, issues which are also a major topic of dicussion in the August 1995 report on academic careers in science by the House of Lords Select Committee on Science and Technology (Ref. 134).

For those scientists tempted to give themselves an unfair advantage in the cut-throat competition for research posts, funding and professional kudos, the traditional organisation and management of research laboratories may offer an ideal environment. Young scientists often work relatively independently, especially in large or prestigious laboratories where senior scientists may spend far more of their time on administration, publicity and fund raising activities than on actual research, a phenomenon which is increasingly likely given the financial constraints and the demands to demonstrate managerial effectiveness which face academic science all over the world (Ref. 129).

Although they will routinely appear as co-authors of research papers, senior scientists may have only a passing acquaintance with the work published in their name. However, the credibility which that name confers will often allow the work of a relatively junior scientist to escape detailed scrutiny at the peer review stage. The John Darsee case is often described as typical in this respect, and many others show similar characteristics. For example the ability of Mark Spector, a brilliant graduate student at Cornell University, to fabricate a whole series of experiments has been attributed to the relative freedom with which he worked. The head of his laboratory, Dr Efraim Racker, was eminent in his field and had numerous outside responsibilities; when Spector's findings were queried by a colleague, Racker had to repeat all of the work which had been published under his name as co-author.

Both factors – the relative working independence of junior scientists, and the vicarious credibility conferred by the senior co-author – can provide a fruitful environment for the potential deceiver, and are a direct result of what Beth Savan describes as the unwritten contract which exists between junior and senior research scientists in the modern laboratory (Ref. 121). The former collect the data, do the research work and draft the publications. The latter set research directions; acquire funding, equipment and other resources; and confer prestige on the work and reputations of juniors by co-authoring their research publications. This in turn, through the process of peer review and quantitative research assessment, forms the basis of the next bid for funding, the next research contract and the next step up the career ladder.

This mutually beneficial relationship is potentially dangerous not simply because it offers opportunities for deception to the young scientist, although it is the need for better supervision and 'mentorship' of juniors which most often exercises the scientific community. Equally important may be the barriers it puts in the way of a junior scientist challenging the work of a superior. If a young scientist's future career is dependent to a very real degree on the patronage of his or her superior, it may prove difficult to question the latter's conduct. It may also be difficult to gain support elsewhere within the institution if that conduct is closely associated with future success in attracting funding.

Anonymous contributors to the recent BBC *Horizon* programme (Ref. 48, Ch. 1) make clear that challenging superiors can be fraught with problems. In one case a young researcher involved in the trials of a new drug noted that his supervisor, who 'had an investment in demonstrating that this particular therapy was effective'...'broke into my filing cabinet and removed the randomisation envelopes [for the assignment of patients to the trial], which had been entrusted to me'. When the junior scientist refused to substitute a patient in a treatment group, there was 'quite a row about it, and he later tried to fire me saying that I wasn't competent'. A second researcher involved in trials of a treatment for AIDS 'found results that were being systematically changed'. On reporting this to his superior he 'found that all sorts of investigations into my own work and performance began'. Needless to say, this kind of anecdotal and anonymous evidence is all too easy for the scientific establishment to ignore.

Commercialism

Much of what has been said so far concerns money – individual salaries, promotion prospects, the next research grant – and many commentators see the commercialisation of the scientific endeavour as the major reason behind the problem of deception. David Miller and Michel Hersen in their study of *Research fraud in the behavioral and biomedical sciences* describe the emergence in the USA of a 'market mentality to research...with academic departments in medical schools often being guided by fiscal considerations rather than academic ones' (Ref. 125). The subtitle of Bell's analysis of *Impure science: fraud, compromise and political influence in scientific research* also suggests the contamination of the scientific endeavour by inappropriate commercial and political pressures (Ref. 126). This is equally (possibly more) applicable to the UK where universities have been under severe funding constraints and taxing administrative pressures for rather longer.

The traditional ivory tower has been assaulted in a number of ways in the past decade and a half: by real terms cuts in public funding at a time when scientific opportunities, and the costs of research, are increasing rapidly; by the requirement to link research activity more closely to the demands of the economy, and to gain a greater proportion of research income from industry; and by the introduction of more rigorous accountability for the expenditure of public money on both teaching and research. The links between academia, government and industry are growing ever closer under the influence of policies which emphasise both the wealth creation potential of science, and the responsibility of public sector bodies to use taxpayers' money effectively. The implications for the integrity of the research process have spawned a substantial literature of their own, in both the UK and abroad. Central to this, for the research community at least, is the basic question of whether a commitment to the pursuit of truth can be reconciled with the concept of science as a commodity.

Few would deny that universities should be required to compete vigorously for funding, which is inevitably limited, and demonstrate that they use it wisely. However, policy makers need to be aware that there could be a price to be paid for requiring scientists to work by the same rules as the rest of the economy. Although it may be true that the scientific endeavour is no different, in essence, from other forms of human activity, it does demand an unusual degree of commitment to the truth which does not respond to financial or managerial stimuli in the same way as, for example, the development of a new product. Indeed, such stimuli may be positively damaging if carried too far. In the words of Dr Richard Broadwell in the *Horizon* programme, 'scientists are like everybody else: they need money to survive, to do their work, and if they don't have those funds they're going to cheat, they're going to lie in order to survive. The fear of failure is rampant in the scientific community' (Ref. 48, Ch. 1).

Fear may well lead to a conservative bias in research, a deliberate preference for areas or methods of work which the researcher knows from experience are likely to attract support. Thus Kuhn's 'normal science' may be given an added boost at the expense of innovative thinking to the eventual detriment of the public good. Of equal concern is the potential impact of financial insecurity (personal or institutional) on the balance between the scientific community's commitment to ethical principles and its desire for survival. While a certain amount of insecurity may be beneficial in stimulating innovative thinking, too much will produce a situation in which monetary rather than scientific issues dominate the research strategy. At the extreme end of this argument lies deliberate deception for financial gain or survival. The policy maker's role is to decide where the balance should lie and one might argue that, in the UK, the shift towards the 'market mentality' has gone too far, or at least too fast.

Pressure from sponsors

Financial insecurity, whether personal or organisational, is only one aspect of the commercialisation of science which might lead to a breach of ethical principles. The intense competition for funding is not simply a reflection of the fight for survival, but a response to the enormous potential rewards to be gained in some areas of science, both for individuals and for organisations (Ref. 123). This is particularly so in biomedical research and it is no accident that many of the reported instances of deception occur in this field with its potentially heady mixture of professional acclaim and social lionisation. In most other areas the pay-out is more limited: the 'discovery' of a complete fossilised archaeopteryx, for example, offers professional status and a certain amount of public interest, but does not compare with the rewards to be won by the developer of an AIDS vaccine or a cure for multiple sclerosis.

These largely personal motivations may be compounded by pressures exerted by the commercial sponsors of research who stand to gain financially from the work of academic scientists. Closer academic-industry links are actively promoted by many governments in order to expand the funding base of science (or fill the gap left by the withdrawal of public funding), and to tie academic research more closely to the needs of the 'real' world. However, there may be unintended consequences of which policy makers should be aware, including the subtle subversion of public sector science to particular commercial interests and the imposition of unacceptable pressures on academic scientists for reasons of profit or competitive edge (Refs. 120, 130).

Corporate funders of academic research generally (though not always) require a return in terms of patentable results in advance of the competition, and this may encourage scientists to cut corners, play down negative research findings or manipulate data in the interests of the quick, positive result. This is needed not only to satisfy the commercial demands of the sponsor, but to ensure the continuation of the research funding relationship. In a world in which universities are having to turn increasingly to the private sector for money, such trade-offs between strict ethical principles and the need to ensure the next research grant may become increasingly common.

In most cases direct financial gain on the part of individual scientists is not an issue, except in so far as deceptive conduct may be linked to promotion or the renewal of a contract. However, it can be a problem in the particular case of clinical drug trials where general practitioners or contract research organisations receive payment for recruiting patients onto trials or generous expenses for attending conferences in sometimes exotic locations (Ref. 124). Another possibility raised by Freestone and Mitchell is illegal share dealing by people who have inside information about the results of clinical trials (Ref. 128). The fact that a drug company's GP researchers are also its customers can make the policing of misconduct very difficult, and there is the additional problem that patient safety may be directly at risk. It is, therefore, not surprising that the Association of the British Pharmaceutical Industry has been particularly active in the development of formal guidelines on the prevention, detection and disciplining of misconduct (Ref. 127)

This discussion of the pressures on scientists suggests, contrary to the traditional view, that personality disorders are very far from the only cause of deceptive behaviour. Certainly professional vanity, 'greed for applause' and other personality traits play a part, but there are a great many other external factors which may encourage deceptive behaviour or reduce the chance of its detection. Some are inherent in the traditional organisation of the scientific endeavour including the hierarchical laboratory system and the pressure to publish. Others derive from policy initiatives designed to make academic science more 'fiscally responsible' (seen by many as a euphemism for funding cuts), and to harness it more closely to the needs of the 'real' world. Clearly, any response to the problem of scientific deception will need to involve not just scientists but policy makers and funding agencies, both private and public.

(120)
SPECIAL section on private appropriation of public research
Science, Technology and Human Values, Winter 1987 12(1) Complete issue
Includes a range of articles on the problems which may arise as a result of closer academic–industry relations. Includes discussion of ethical issues as well as practical problems relating to intellectual property rights.

(121)
SCIENCE under siege: the myth of objectivity in scientific research
Savan, B
CBC Enterprises: Montreal, 1988. 192pp
An 'unashamedly partisan' analysis of the scientific process which aims to expose the vested interests (personal, organisational and political) which influence science and scientists in the real world. Looks at self-deception and deliberate misconduct, giving

illustrations from many well known cases and identifying influential factors. These include the pressure to publish, to gain academic recognition and to satisfy the demands of private interests.

(122)
A MATTER of integrity
Petersdorf, R G
Academic Medicine, Mar 1989 64(3) pp119-23, 14 references
Argues that fraud and misconduct have become major problems for science and medicine, with academic pressures a major contributing factor. These include the pressure to excel, to produce, to publish, to achieve tenure and to be promoted.

(123)
HUMAN genetics information: science, law and ethics: Ciba Foundation symposium
Wiley: Chichester, Mar 1990. 211pp
A collection of papers on the scientific, legal and ethical issues surrounding research on genetic manipulation, an area of biotechnology in which there is tremendous pressure for commercial exploitation.

(124)
BIOMEDICAL information, peer review and conflict of interest as they influence public health
Cantekin, E I and others
Journal of the American Medical Association, 9 Mar 1990 263(10) pp1427-30
Discusses potential conflicts of interest in drug research paid for by large companies. Although companies may not offer direct payments to individuals, they do provide ample research funding, resources for conference attendance, lecture fees etc. Also the attraction of such funding can enhance the researcher's reputation with his university. Suggests that this may lead to experimental bias.

(125)
ACADEMIC pressures
Thelen, M H and Di Lorenzo, T M
In: Research fraud in the behavioral and biomedical sciences, edited by D J Miller and
    M Hersen
      Wiley: Chichester, 1992 pp161-81, 67 references
Presents definitions of research fraud, assesses its prevalence, and looks at the extent of stress and pressure in academia. Relevant factors include the pressure to publish as a means of academic and professional advancement; and excessive workloads. For further comment in Miller and Hersen's book on how these pressures, and others such as the growth of academic 'entrepreneurship' can be addressed
See also: Future directions: a modest proposal, by M Hersen and D J Miller (pp225-41, 31 references)

(126)
IMPURE science: fraud, compromise, and political influence in scientific research
Bell, R
Wiley: New York, 1992. 301pp, 585 references
Bell's 'primary purpose is to show that the American scientific community is as "pure"

and unbiased as the political machinery that dispenses its patronage and its funding'. Argues that certain members of the scientific community 'have encouraged a trend towards political influence, compromise and fraud in scientific research' while the majority of the scientific community has looked the other way.

(127)

A PHARMACEUTICAL company's approach to the threat of research fraud
Brock, P
In: Fraud and misconduct in medical research, edited by S Lock and F Wells
    BMJ Publishing: London, 1993 pp25-41, 3 references
Identifies some of the reasons why researchers engaged in clinical trials might commit fraud, and looks at the difficulties facing pharmacuetical companies in tackling the problem; in particular the fact that the company's researchers (GPs and other practising doctors) are often also its customers. Cites a number of cases and looks at ways of detecting and prosecuting fraud. For more on the relationship between the pharmaceutical industry and the research community in Lock and Wells' book
See also: Fraud and general practice research: intention to cheat, by J Hosie (pp42-49) The pharmaceutical industry and contract research organisations, by M Vandenburg and others (pp50-60)

(128)

INAPPROPRIATE publication of trial results and potential for allegations of illegal share dealing
Freestone, D S and Mitchell, H
British Medical Journal, 24 Apr 1993 306(6885) pp1112-14, 22 references
Argues that there is increasing evidence of fraud in clinical research, including the illegal trading in drug company shares by researchers with inside information on the results of trials. Pressure may also be exerted for the premature or inappropriate communication of research results.

(129)

GRADUATE education in Britain
Becher, T and others
Jessica Kingsley: London, 1994. 214pp
A study based on an analysis of national trends and detailed case studies of small, medium and large research centres in 18 universities. Covers the natural sciences (physics and biochemistry), the social sciences (economics and sociology) and the humanities (history and modern languages). Notes the inadequate support and supervision of many young postgraduate researchers.

(130)

ACADEMIC-industry relations: special issue
Science and Public Policy, Apr 1994 21(2) pp70-120
A special issue coinciding with the establishment of an International Study Group to explore the issue of academic-industry collaboration in the wider innovation process. Includes a select bibliography by Kathryn Packer. For another journal special issue which also includes a select, annotated bibliography covering the period 1987-1993
See also: University-industry-government cooperation (International Journal of Technology Management, 1993 8(6/7/8) Complete issue)

(131)

INDEPENDENT investigators and for-profit companies: guidelines for biomedical scientists considering funding by industry

Chren, M M

Archives of Dermatology, Apr 1994 130(4) pp432-37, 25 references

The scientist's traditional independence to define and pursue scientific goals is increasingly under threat from external pressures. Looks at instances in which accountabilities may conflict, and sets out detailed guidelines including (first and foremost) the need for a proper contractual relationship between the scientist and the external funder.

(132)

SOUNDING board: institutional conflict of interest

Emanuel, E J and Steiner, D

New England Journal of Medicine, 26 Jan 1995 332(4) pp262-67, 36 references

Considers the problem of conflicts of interest in the biomedical field using a case that arose at a hospital affiliated to Harvard University. Develops a framework for analysing such conflicts, identifies their potential dangers, and looks at ways in which these might be avoided or minimised.

(133)

SCIENCE and engineering in the universities: quality at risk

Save British Science Society, Box 241, Oxford OX1 3QQ, Apr 1995. 35pp
(SBS Memorandum)

A memorandum to the Department for Education in the context of its review of higher education. Includes comment on the rapid growth of short-term contract working among university research scientists. For more on this issue

See also: Contract researchers: the human resource, by C Varlaam (University of Sussex Institute of Manpower (now Employment) Studies, Mantell Building, Falmer, Brighton BN1 9RF, Feb 1988. 51pp)

Commitment betrayed: a survey of contract research staff in UK universities (Association of University Teachers, 9 Pembridge Road, London W11 3JY, 1994. 6pp)

(134)

ACADEMIC research careers for graduate scientists: 4th report, session 1994–95

House of Lords Select Committee on Science and Technology

HMSO, Aug 1995. 2 volumes (HL60, 60-I)

Includes extensive discussion of the problems facing contract research staff, and makes recommendations to improve their terms and conditions of service. For brief comment on a proposed agreement on these issues by the Royal Society, the Committee of Vice Chancellors and Principals, the research councils and the Office of Science and Technology

See also: Contract researchers glimpse future, by K Patel (Times Higher, 28 Jul 1995 (1186) p5)

3. RESPONSES AND POLICY IMPLICATIONS

Much of the literature referred to so far, and most of the cases, are American, and it is in the United States that the issues relating to scientific deception have been discussed most exhaustively. It is also here that the greatest effort has been put into developing effective responses at both government and institutional level. Observers elsewhere in the world have sometimes comforted themselves by claiming that deception is a uniquely American problem, perhaps fostered by a more competitive and materialist culture or by the particular nature of the academic environment. Such beliefs are probably illusory. The practice of science differs little across national boundaries, and the environment in which scientists work is shaped by a number of common factors in the advanced countries.

There is an increasing convergence in science policies fuelled by the realisation that the potential for scientific advance far outstrips the resources of even the wealthiest nation. Academic science is facing steady state or declining funding in real terms in many countries as governments struggle to reduce public sector deficits, and scientists are increasingly required to demonstrate value for money in the expenditure of those funds they do receive. At the same time, governments are searching for a rational basis on which to justify funding only a fraction of the work of which the scientific community is capable. In most cases this focuses on wealth creation and the linking of the scientific endeavour to industrial competitiveness. Secondary objectives may include, as in the British case, improvements in quality of life.

Although the importance of undirected blue-skies research is still stressed by policy makers, there is a sense in the scientific community that this is little more than rhetorical homage to the past. Traditional ivory tower basic research is on the defensive in a world where industrial relevance, managerial efficiency and the entrepreneurial spirit are seen as the keystones of effective modern science (Ref. 136). Science is now firmly in the 'real' world and inextricably interwined with both government and the private sector. This puts the traditional practice of science, encapsulated in the notion of the disinterested pursuit of truth, under pressure in at least two ways.

Science under pressure

On the one hand, science is increasingly important to society for the physical and mental health of individuals and for current and future economic well-being. A commitment to truth is thus of direct relevance to policy makers, industrial users of research and ordinary people, and all are likely to attach increasing importance to ethical conduct within the laboratory. On the other hand, the explicit linking of the scientific endeavour to social and economic goals, particularly those relating to competitiveness, carries with it the risk that the pursuit of truth may be compromised in the interests of reaching those goals before others do so. If this conflict is played out in a situation of public funding constraints and pressure on academic departments to gain a higher proportion of their income from private interests, the chances of compromise may be all the greater.

It is for these reasons that scientific deception should be an important issue within science policy. It matters not just to science, or to those individuals caught up unwittingly in particular cases, but to everyone in an increasingly science and technology-dependent world. It is, of course, important for research institutions, the scientific publishing world and funding bodies to develop ways of detecting misconduct, punishing it, and eradicating its effects. It is also important that effective programmes of ethical training for young scientists are developed and that whistleblowers are protected from unfair attack or discrimination.

However, it is equally vital that those with responsibility for planning the future shape and direction of science are fully aware of the pressures their decisions may impose on working scientists. The scientific establishment also needs to accept publicly that its traditional values may not always be proof against radical change of the kind imposed in recent years. It is no longer possible for either party to assume that the disinterested pursuit of truth will survive the collapse of the ivory tower, if only because the public already suspects that it has not. Far better for all concerned to admit that science is as potentially vulnerable to ethical compromise as other activities, not just because of the impositions of government and private interests but because of its own internal dynamics.

The remainder of this chapter looks at how the issues have been addressed in the United States and, to a much lesser extent, elsewhere. However, even in the USA, one might argue that the response is largely one of locking the stable door after the horse has bolted, or of dealing with the effects rather than the causes of the problem. Although increasing attention is being paid to the ethical training of young scientists, and to the problems resulting from conflicts of interest between academia and industry, most interest focuses on the definition of misconduct and the development of institutional responses to the detection and disciplining of wrong-doing. These are clearly necessary, but even more might be achieved by concentrating on those factors which may encourage deceptive behaviour in the first place and make it difficult to challenge.

A radical response

Of the analyses covered in this review, Beth Savan's *Science under siege* is one of the few to take this broader view and she is dealing principally with the issue of bias in research which she clearly sees as even more damaging to the public good than outright misconduct (Ref. 135). Simply re-stating her proposals is perhaps all that is needed to explain why politicians and scientists prefer to concentrate on effects rather than causes:

> 'First, we should all accept that bias unavoidably alters scientific research, and we should develop measures to challenge the biases of investigators.'

> 'Second, we should take steps to disengage, as much as possible, the scientists doing research from the vested interests that have a stake in its outcome.'

The practical implications of these simple statements are profound. They do, of course, involve the introduction of 'institutionalized protocols and public penalties for malpractice...to discourage obvious distortion of research results to favour friends, patrons, political allies, or personal careers'; improvements in the education and mentoring of young scientists; and detailed attention to the deficiencies of the scientific publishing system. However, they also challenge the basis of government science policies designed to bring academia and industry closer together, and to increase the proportion of funding derived from private sector sources. Equally they involve explicit criticism of the hierarchical organisation of the scientific endeavour, and the operation of patronage and discrimination through the peer review system.

In Savan's view a healthy scientific system openly recognises that the influence of vested interests (personal, professional, institutional and political) is inevitable, and seeks to reduce it by dilution and the glare of publicity. It is pluralist, transparent and egalitarian; encourages young researchers to challenge scientific orthodoxy; actively welcomes involvement by the public and interest groups; and seeks the widest possible range of scientific opinion in the development of policies. It demands mandatory public disclosure by all academic scientists of their commercial, governmental and other affiliations when applying for funding, acting as peer reviewers or serving on policy committees; and it requires universities and other institutions to develop detailed guidelines on conflicts of interest.

In short, it challenges virtually every principle held dear by the scientific establishment, and threatens the 'wealth creation' basis of most contemporary science policies in so far as they seek to promote a greater degree of entrepreneurialism in science. As such the practical chances of Beth Savan seeing her proposals implemented must be slight although her analysis of the pressures on science should give far-sighted policy makers food for thought.

(135)
CONCLUSIONS
B Savan
In: Science under siege: the myth of objectivity in scientific research, by B Savan
    CBC Enterprises: Montreal, 1988 pp145-57

(136)
THE RESEARCH university in a time of discontent
Cole, J R and others
Johns Hopkins University Press: Baltimore, MD, Jan 1995. 320pp
There have been a number of studies of the crisis which many American academics feel is facing the research university system as a result of funding restrictions and conflicts of interest between the academic enterprise and private business. This is one of the most recent. For others
See also: In the national interest: the federal government and research-intensive universities (National Science Foundation: Washington, DC, 1992. 59pp)
Renewing the promise: research-intensive universities and the nation (President's Council of Advisors on Science and Technology: Washington, DC, 1992. 69pp)
Research and relevant knowledge: American research universities since World War II, by R L Geiger (Oxford University Press, 1993. 411pp)
The fragile contract: university science and the federal government, edited by D H Guston and K Keniston (MIT Press, Oct 1994. 270pp)

3.1 United States

The experience of the United States in addressing the issue of scientific deception has much to offer the rest of the world, even though its academic, legal and political cultures may differ. Modern interest is often dated from the William Summerlin affair of the mid-1970s, or from the publication of the Edsall Report in 1975. This dealt principally with allegations made by two whistleblowers about standards of safety in the United States Atomic Energy Commission, but has remained an important general statement on the social obligations of the scientist in the modern world (Ref. 137). It concluded that scientists have a primary right and responsibility to blow the whistle when they encounter misconduct. In 1981 a further report on whistleblowing, this time in the biomedical sciences, was published by the President's Commission for the Study of Ethical Problems in Medicine and Biomedical and Behavioral Research (Ref. 139).

Congressional worries

During the late 1970s and early 1980s, as already noted in Chapter 2, the number of reported cases of biomedical misconduct associated with the National Institutes of Health and the Food and Drug Administration increased substantially. Prompted by growing public alarm, the House Committee on Science and Technology convened hearings by the Subcommittee on Investigations and Oversight in the Spring of 1981 under the chairmanship of Al Gore (Ref. 138). Patricia Woolf's analysis of the hearings (Ref. 26, Ch. 1) shows in detail how the scientific community employed defensive tactics to rebut charges that misconduct was widespread, and assure the Subcommittee that it was well able to handle the rare cases which did occur.

Nonetheless, the American Association of Medical Colleges felt it necessary to issue guidelines on ethical standards in 1982 which confirmed the Edsall Report's views on whistleblowers and developed a three stage procedure for the investigation of allegations at institutional level. This emphasised the importance of due process, or protecting the rights of all parties involved in investigations (Ref. 140). Six years later the Association of American Universities produced a similar framework, with additional recommendations to ensure that investigations were carried out confidentially, within a laid down timescale, and by people who were expert but with no personal interest in the cases in which they were involved (Ref. 147).

However, despite these measures, Congressional worries about the incidence of scientific misconduct persisted in the face of yet more scandals. A whole series of hearings was held during the 1980s, later ones under the chairmanship of John Dingell who has been tireless in his pursuit of wrong-doers and described by one science journalist (in an admiring context, it should be said) as 'a political vulture, circling for prey'. By 1985 Congress had lost patience with the scientific community's response to the problem and enacted s493 of the Public Health Service Act. This required the Secretary of Health and Human Services to issue rules demanding that institutions in receipt of public research funding establish 'an administrative process to review reports of scientific fraud' and 'report to the Secretary any investigation of alleged fraud which appears substantial' (Ref. 160).

Some individual universities established procedures in response to this stimulus but many still remained unconvinced of the need for formal procedures (Ref. 142). The National Institutes of Health also amended its *Guide for grants and contracts* in July 1986 to include details of its own procedures for dealing with allegations (Ref. 143). However, these did little more than record the *ad hoc* methods which the NIH had already been using in the firm belief that the informal resolution of problems between gentlemen (or ladies) was the most effective approach. The NIH also announced the introduction of a computer system, ALERT, which contained details of all scientists under investigation which were passed to NIH personnel for use in decision making on the granting of awards or posts.

During the same period, measures were also being implemented at the Food and Drug Administration to deal with its own increase in cases of reported misconduct in clinical drug trials. The FDA chose a rigorous, quasi-judicial procedure based on data audits and formal trial-like hearings. These had considerable success in reducing the incidence of misconduct in clinical trials and, though data audits may be inappropriate for the kinds of research funded by the NIH, the trial process was seen as an eminently practical alternative to the informal procedures still favoured by many in the academic community (Refs. 55, 62, Ch. 2).

The belief that these procedures were inadequate was also gaining ground in the wake of more Congressional hearings during 1988 and 1989 into the ability of the NIH to deal effectively with allegations including those in the Baltimore case (Refs. 145, 149, 151). Congressional interest in specific cases has continued, for example with hearings in 1991 on the case of Robert Gallo, accused of making false statements in four papers on the AIDS virus published in *Science* (Ref. 159). This political 'interference' has not infrequently aroused the ire of the scientific community.

NIH responses

Following the Baltimore hearing it was widely reported that John Dingell and other Congressmen were contemplating draconian legislation to police the scientific community in the absence of effective self-regulation. The Department of Health and Human Services attempted to head off this intervention by codifying the procedures laid down in the NIH *Guide* and making them more rigorous, but it was soon evident that this was not enough either for Congress or concerned elements within the scientific community.

The Institute of Medicine's 1989 report on *The responsible conduct of research in the health sciences* was particularly influential and called on the NIH to establish a new office to ensure proper research conduct, and to require all federally funded institutions to establish investigatory mechanisms (Ref. 148). The Department compromised by creating two new offices: the Office of Scientific Integrity within the NIH, to be responsible for monitoring university investigations and undertaking its own where necessary; and the Office of Scientific Integrity Review within the Department itself to be responsible for reviewing OSI investigations and recommending appropriate sanctions to the Secretary of Health and Human Services.

The OSI/OSIR framework was unstable from the start. There were no published rules governing the objectives or conduct of either office, in contrast to the detailed requirements imposed on universities by rules published in August 1989 (Ref. 152). In practice the OSI continued to work using the traditional 'scientific dialogue' process in which witnesses could be interviewed, evidence assessed and penalties imposed, all without the due process which was widely accepted as an essential characteristic of an effective and fair system. Although Director Jules Hallum and his deputy Suzanne Hadley defended the use of scientific dialogue in their assessment of the OSI's first year, it was widely criticised for slowness, secrecy, susceptibility to political influence, and unfairness because of a lack of due process (Ref. 154). As an embodiment of the traditional scientific approach to dealing with misconduct, it proved strikingly unpopular with scientists themselves.

Matters were finally resolved in the wake of the James Abbs affair in which Abbs and his university argued before the courts that the OSI could not arrive at a verdict on his alleged misconduct without allowing him due process. The judge not only agreed with this claim but ruled that all OSI policies and procedures were illegal because there had been no publication of procedures governing its conduct, and no opportunity for public comment upon them. A subsequent appeal against this decision by both sides found against Abbs on both counts, but the days of the OSI and OSIR were numbered (Ref. 168).

Office of Research Integrity

In the summer of 1992 the Office of Scientific Integrity was closed, and its functions transferred out of the National Institutes of Health into the parent Department of Health and Human Services which was seen as further removed from the scientific community and thus more likely to foster impartiality. A new Office of Research Integrity was created, combining the staff and functions of both the OSI and OSIR, but with an improved definition and separation of duties. The investigative division carries out the functions of the old OSI but its reports contain only results and recommended conclusions rather than final decisions on whether misconduct has taken place. In cases where there is a proposed finding of misconduct, the researcher can ask for a special appeal hearing, with due process protection, by a board including both scientific and legal expertise (Refs. 169, 170).

The definition of scientific misconduct used by the ORI is relatively limited in practical terms – 'fabrication, falsification, plagiarism, or other practices that seriously deviate from those that are commonly accepted within the scientific community for proposing, conducting or reporting research'. Since few people can agree on what 'other practices' might be, the focus is almost exclusively on 'FF&P' although the ORI is now also turning its attention to the investigation of alleged retaliation against whistleblowers. Since its establishment, the ORI has heard more than 200 cases but its more adversarial and legalistic approach has not always been successful. Several cases such as that against Mikulas Popovic (accused, like Robert Gallo, of making false statements about the AIDS virus) have been overturned at the appeal stage for want of evidence, and the ORI dropped its charges against Gallo in late 1993 in the expectation of a similar verdict. Meanwhile, the long-running Baltimore/Imanishi-Kari saga is still unresolved. The ORI appeal board hearing during the summer of 1995 is expected to take several weeks to examine the 19 charges of misconduct filed against Thereza Imanishi-Kari in connection with a research paper that is now nine years old.

Significant problems are associated with the establishment of proof in this and other complex cases. The ORI is required by the appeals board to prove intentional deception in order to distinguish between misconduct and honest error, and to show that any mis-statement of fact has a 'material' effect on the validity of the scientist's results. Neither are simple matters. Nor is there complete agreement on what constitutes misconduct, even within the terms of the restrictive 'FF&P' definition. For example, the ORI's latest annual report notes the difficulties it has faced in dealing with alleged plagiarism despite its own detailed operational definition (Ref. 184). In practice, most complaints of plagiarism have turned out to be disputes about authorship or credit.

It is perhaps interesting to note that one of the most recent cases of plagiarism has been resolved without any recourse to the ORI (Ref. 187). Pamela Berge, a former epidemiologist at Cornell University, filed a suit against four researchers at the University of Alabama accusing them of stealing her PhD thesis work on cytomegalovirus infections in newborn children and passing it off as their own. She used the False Claims Act, a piece of legislation that allows private citizens who allege that government contractors have made a false claim to bring a *qui tam* suit on behalf of the government, and won a verdict that could cost the University and its researchers very dearly. Berge herself was awarded $265,000 in compensatory and punitive damages, and is entitled to 30% of the $1.65 million to be paid to the government.

There is some unease among misconduct experts that this case could prompt others to bypass the carefully constructed ORI edifice which still, despite its legalistic trappings, allows the scientific community a significant measure of control over its own activities. Cases which demonstrate that the mainstream legal system, and lay juries, are quite capable of reaching reasoned judgements in scientific misconduct cases will do yet more to dent the perception that science and scientists are somehow different and should be treated by different rules from everyone else.

In particular, they will hearten lawyers like the US attorney who prosecuted in the case of Stephen Breuning, accused of falsifying evidence about the impact on severely retarded children of the removal of certain tranquillisers from their treatment programmes. Breuning's prosecutor had to face criticism from the scientific community that 'criminal indictment' and 'legislative oversight' of its activities would dissuade people from entering research (Ref. 163). His response – 'hogwash' – is echoed rather more soberly by Pamela Berge's lawyer who said that her case 'revolved not around complex scientific concepts but around basic questions of honesty and intellectual property. The jury understood it and gave us a very measured verdict. It's an example of science working in the courtroom'.

Some policy lessons from the USA

The complex story of American responses to the misconduct issue is useful for scientists and policy makers in other countries both for the wealth of published information it provides about the nature and causes of scientific deception, and for the lessons it offers about how deception might be approached as a policy issue. It makes clear that self-policing through the traditional method of 'scientific dialogue' is not a realistic option once scientific misconduct has become a major issue of public concern. Not only does it fail to satisfy public and political demands for accountability, it can be deeply unpopular among accused scientists themselves if there is a lack of due process. If there is to be some form of independent investigatory authority, it clearly has to operate by formal rules which everyone recognises as fair. The same arguments apply to investigatory procedures at the institutional level.

However, while these procedures need to be designed within the framework of legal principle, and implemented with legal advice, recourse to the civil or criminal law itself is often not a realistic option. In the United States, as the Berge case shows most recently, some perpetrators of fraud have been successfully prosecuted through the courts, and there continue to be discussions about the applicability of criminal proceedings to allegations which have been substantiated by a process of scientific inquiry (Ref. 161). However, in many respects the practical problems faced by the American courts in dealing with scientific misconduct are likely to be repeated in other countries. It is quite possible, for example, that a British court faced with a case as complex as the Baltimore/Imanishi-Kari affair would react, as the US legal system did – by throwing up its hands in despair, claiming that no jury would be capable of assessing the evidence and concluding that such cases 'ought to be left to scientists'. Moreover, as noted in Chapter 1, many kinds of scientific misconduct violate no laws at all.

It might be also be argued that public court proceedings are inappropriate in cases of suspected scientific misconduct because of the damage which can be caused to professional reputations both by the act of whistleblowing and by the need to defend unsubstantiated allegations. According to this view, investigatory procedures and safeguards should be within the public domain but proceedings should be confidential, at least at the institutional level. Only when guilt or innocence has been established by a process of quasi-legal scientific inquiry will publicity be appropriate to vindicate a whistleblower's actions, attest to the reputation of the falsely accused, or submit a proven fraudster to professional discipline or criminal proceedings.

Breaking down resistance

A further lesson which the American experience offers to the policy maker is its demonstration of the strength of the academic community's self-protective instincts, its ability to stonewall, and its resentment of outside interference. Allan Mazur in his 1989 analysis of American universities' responses to allegations of dishonesty notes that many were slow to react to the changes in rules introduced by the NIH in 1986. By 1988 only 22% of institutions receiving NIH funding had established formal procedures although this figure did include the vast majority of large research centres receiving 100 or more grants (Ref. 150). However, the Institute of Medicine in its 1989 report claimed that such procedures were rarely comprehensive, with omissions such as failing to require the institution to notify the NIH of allegations (Ref. 148).

In 1990, well after the issuing of guidelines by the NIH, the Association of American Universities and others, the House Committee on Government Operations investigated the circumstances of ten cases of misconduct at Harvard, Yeshiva University and the universities of Florida, Pittsburgh, and California (San Diego). It was highly critical of the universities' 'reluctance' to find faculty members guilty, their inadequate investigative procedures, and their retaliation against whistleblowers. However, it is indicative of the passions that these issues arouse that the report was not unanimous. There were dissenting minority views on the accuracy of the data quoted, the recommendations and the 'questionable' intervention of Congress in such an area (Ref. 153).

The reluctance of universities to institute formal procedures for investigating and dealing with misconduct was also noted by Joel Nobel in another analysis published in 1990 (Ref. 156). A survey of medical schools in the United States and Canada showed that only two of the 133 responding schools had formal guidelines in place, in marked contrast to the findings of a parallel study focusing on non-academic institutions. Many of these had policy and procedure documents dealing with issues such as the ethical and moral framework of research, and institutional responsibility for research done by individuals. Perhaps even more worrying is evidence that whistleblowers continue to suffer despite the Whistleblower Protection Act 1989 and other relevant legislation although, to be fair to science, it is not the only community at fault in this respect (Refs. 171).

The apparent unwillingness of the American scientific community to put its own house in order casts doubt on whether improved self-policing can ever be a realistic alternative to greater external oversight, although this approach continues to be promoted (Ref. 177). It is equally doubtful whether anything effective can be done without the concerted intervention of committed individuals within the scientific community and government. It is, for example, interesting to speculate on what the American situation might be without the tenacious pursuit of misconduct as a policy issue by John Dingell, former chairman of the House of Representatives Subcommittee on Oversight and Investigations, and other members of the legislature. Dingell's willingness to speak out, for example in the 1992 Shattuck Lecture, and to suffer the inevitable onslaught of criticism was instrumental in pushing the scientific community towards recognising and addressing the misconduct problem (Ref. 173).

This is not to say that there is a lack of interest among American academic scientists in the problem or an unwillingness to discuss it. Nor is there any lack of innovative thinking on how it might be approached in policy or procedural terms. The difficulty seems to lie in translating ideas into action, particularly at the institutional level. This may be the result of a mismatch in views between the mass of the scientific community and those individuals at the forefront of developing responses to the misconduct issue, although the results of opinion surveys noted in Chapter 2 appear to belie this. Many ordinary scientists seem to be concerned, but what they cannot stomach is the idea that non-scientific outsiders (politicians, investigative journalists, lawyers, 'professional' whistleblowers) could have a role to play.

Perhaps it is the very complexity of the issues — for example how to define misconduct or assess evidence of it — which paralyses the efforts of scientists to address the problem themselves and makes it so difficult for them to accept that others can play a part. Perhaps it is something to do with the university environment, or simply a strong distaste for washing dirty linen in public. Whatever the reason, there is a very real sense that the American scientific community would have remained bogged down in its own agonising over the problems without the pressures exerted by Dingell and his colleagues.

A willingness to talk

Nonetheless, that agonising has produced much which might be of use to scientific communities and policy makers outside the United States. It has, moreover, been a public process involving a wide range of participants which contrasts starkly with the almost complete silence in most other countries. The National Academy of Sciences, National Academy of Engineering and the Institute of Medicine set up a major study in 1989 on the responsible conduct of science which resulted in a two volume report published in 1992 and 1993 examining the issue from almost every conceivable angle (Refs. 165, 166). In the same year the National Academy issued guidance *On being a scientist* which identified a range of unethical behaviours and advised on conduct.

It claimed that 'of all the violations of the ethos of science, fraud is the gravest' but that 'science could not be the successful institution it is if fraud were common'. Emphasis was placed on the publication system as a key regulatory mechanism, and young scientists were advised to look to their seniors for guidance. This allegedly produced hollow laughter among some young scientists who suspected that unethical conduct was at least as rife in the higher echelons of science as in the lower, and the guidance was reissued in amended form in 1995 (Ref. 186). Further practical advice is available to scientists from Sigma Xi, the Scientific Research Society, in *Honor in science* (Ref. 157).

The American Association for the Advancement of Science has also been active, especially through the National Conference of Lawyers and Scientists, a joint body of the AAAS and the American Bar Association founded in 1974. In 1988 and 1989 it reported on three workshops which discussed a wide range of misconduct issues with particular reference to legal and quasi-legal matters, and the development of institutional responses to misconduct (Ref. 144). The AAAS also hosted a media roundtable at the

National Press Club in June 1989 and a two-day conference in late 1991 to promote wider discussion of the issues (Refs. 155, 158). Finally, in March 1992, it published a short report on *Good science and responsible scientists* which tries to encapsulate the knowledge and experience gained during the investigations of the previous four years (Ref. 167). Since then it has focused on the practicalities of responding to allegations of misconduct, running two workshops in 1993 and 1994 under the aegis of the National Conference of Lawyers and Scientists (Ref. 178), and developing a range of educational videos on scientific research integrity.

Another focus for discussion has been the Institutional Review Board, responsible for monitoring research involving human subjects which is funded from the Department of Health and Human Services. It works within a framework laid down by federal regulation and seeks to ensure a balance between the patient's rights to dignity and self-determination and the overall social benefit to be derived from research involving human subjects. The IRB also publishes its own journal which has included several influential articles over the years on the nature of misconduct and responses to it (Ref. 164).

The American scientific community has not just confined its energies to talking about the problems although, as already noted, it has been cautious in its development of institutional procedures for investigating and disciplining misconduct. However, progress is being made in this direction, with universities such as Harvard in the forefront (Ref. 182). The Association of American Universities has also published a framework document on the problem of conflicts of interest in academic–industry relationships (Ref. 172), an issue which has been taken up more recently by the National Institutes of Health and the National Science Foundation in new rules for award recipients (Ref. 188). Some individual universities are active in designing courses to teach the responsible conduct of research, and the American Association of Medical Colleges has published guidance on the teaching of ethical conduct which relies heavily on a case study approach (Refs. 179, 180, 183). Most recently, the American Medical Association has issued its *Code of medical ethics: current opinions with annotations* which covers both the delivery of health care and the conduct of medical research (Ref. 185). Although the United States may still be concentrating on locking the stable door, it is making some valiant attempts to prevent the horse from bolting in the first place.

(137)
SCIENTIFIC responsibility and freedom
Edsall, J T
American Association for the Advancement of Science, 1333 H Street NW,
Washington, DC 20005, 1975. 50pp, 60 references
The report of the AAAS Committee on Scientific Freedom and Responsibility, issued in response to the allegations of whistleblowers about safety standards at the US Atomic Energy Commission, but regarded as an important analysis of the social responsibilities of scientists in general.

(138)
FRAUD in biomedical research: hearings, 1 Apr–31 May 1981
US Congress House Committee on Science and Technology, Subcommittee on Investigations and Oversight
US Government Printing Office: Washington, DC, 1981. 380pp (Hearings, 97th Congress, 1st session [No. 11])

The first major Congressional hearing on the problem of misconduct in biomedical research which looks at developments in the National Institutes of Health and the Food and Drug Administration.

(139)
Whistleblowing in biomedical research: policies and procedures for responding to reports of misconduct: proceedings of a workshop held on September 21-22 1981
Swazey, J P and Scher, S R (editors)
US Government Printing Office: Washington, DC, 1981. 210pp
A report of the President's Commission for the Study of Ethical Problems in Medicine and Biomedical and Behavioral Research. Argues that incomplete or inaccurate research data, and violations of regulations, can pose serious risks to research subjects. Fraudulent research can also place future patients at risk if it affects decisions on the abandonment or adoption of particular treatments. More fundamentally, it damages science both by diverting scientists down blind alleys and by damaging public confidence.

(140)
THE MAINTENANCE of high ethical standards in the conduct of research
Association of American Medical Colleges
Journal of Medical Education, Nov 1982 57(11) pp895-902
Emphasises the importance of protecting the rights and reputations of all parties involved in cases of alleged misconduct, including whistleblowers. Looks in detail at institutional responses, and recommends a three stage formal investigatory process.

(141)
COMMENTARY: the university and research ethics
Steneck, N H
Science, Technology and Human Values, Fall 1984 9(4) pp6-15, 13 notes and references
Deals with the guidelines issued by the Association of American Medical Colleges, and those of the University of Michigan where Nicholas Steneck is Professor of History. Expresses some unease at the lack of effort to define or survey the misconduct problem, the continuing weakness of peer review, and a certain level of complacency in the research community which believes that the problem will disappear once policing mechanisms are in place. The University of Michigan's guidelines on *Maintaining the integrity of scholarship*, published in 1984, are an attempt to develop a positive, rather than simply policing, approach to misconduct.

(142)
POLICIES for responding to allegations of fraud in research
Greene, P J and others
Minerva, Summer 1985 23(2) pp203-15: a further version is also published under the title *Institutional policies for responding to allegations of research fraud* (IRB: A Review of Human Subjects Research, Jul/Aug 1986 8(4) pp1-7, 16 notes and references)
The analysis shows that some university and medical school administrators remain unconvinced by the case for formal procedures, believing that deception is still best dealt with in the traditional manner. For guidelines issued by individual universities and published in this, and succeeding, issues of *Minerva*
See also: Policy for dealing with faculty fraud in research: University of Florida (Minerva, Summer 1985 23(2) pp305-08)
Report of the Committee on Academic Fraud: the University of Chicago (Minerva,

Summer/Autumn 1986 24(2/3) pp347-58)
The morality of scientists 1: procedures for responding to charges of unethical research practices. The morality of scientists II: report of the faculty ad hoc committee to investigate research fraud, 30 September 1986, by University of California, San Diego School of Medicine (Minerva, Winter 1987 25(4) pp502-12)

(143)
POLICIES and procedures for dealing with possible misconduct in science: NIH guide for grants and contracts, Vol. 15, No. 11: special issue
US Public Health Service
National Institutes of Health: Bethesda, MD 20892, 18 Jul 1986. 37pp
Issued in response to increasing Congressional and public disquiet over misconduct. Requires institutions applying for support from the NIH to adopt formal procedures for investigating misconduct.

(144)
PROJECT on scientific fraud and misconduct: report on workshop number one
National Conference of Lawyers and Scientists
American Association for the Advancement of Science, 1333 H Street NW, Washington, DC 20005, 1988. 136pp, 36 notes and references
The reports of the NCLS workshops focus particularly on self-regulation within the universities and on the application of civil and criminal law to scientific misconduct. For the remaining reports
See also: Project on scientific fraud and misconduct: report on workshop number two (AAAS, 1989. 151pp)
Project on scientific fraud and misconduct: report on workshop number three (AAAS, 1989. 249pp)

(145)
SCIENTIFIC fraud and misconduct and the federal response: hearing, 11 April 1988
US Congress House Committee on Government Operations, Human Resources and Intergovernmental Relations Subcommittee
US Government Printing Office: Washington, 1988. 229pp
Includes discussion of scientific attitudes and the nature of deception, the role of the federal government and institutions in responding to misconduct, the editorial policies of scientific journals and peer review. Also comments on the Jeffrey Borer and Stephen Breuning cases.

(146)
RESPONDING to scientific misconduct: due process and prevention
Mishkin, B
Journal of the American Medical Association, 7 Oct 1988 260(13) pp1932-36, 32 references
Argues that the imposition of stricter penalties for scientific misconduct demands additional due process protection in disciplinary proceedings at the institutional level. These should include adequate publicising of accepted standards of conduct and the sanctions which may be imposed for breaching them; procedural protections during the investigation and hearing; and mechanisms for restoring the reputations of those scientists who are cleared of charges against them. Academic institutions have an important responsibility to be open about admitted or confirmed instances of misconduct.

(147)
FRAMEWORK for institutional policies and procedures to deal with fraud in research
Association of American Universities, National Association of State Universities and Land Grant Colleges, and Council of Graduate Schools
Association of American Universities, One Davenport Circle NW, Washington, DC 20036, Nov 1988. 10pp
Follows the pattern laid down by the Association of American Medical Colleges in emphasising due process, and also adds recommendations relating to confidentiality, expeditiousness, the neutrality of expert investigators and an appeals process.

(148)
THE RESPONSIBLE conduct of research in the health sciences: report of a study
Institute of Medicine Division of Health Sciences Policy, Committee on the Responsible Conduct of Science
National Academy Press: Washington, DC, 1989. 97pp, bibliography pp43-58
(IOM Publication 89-01)
An influential study which finds that institutional or environmental factors can play a part in scientific misconduct as well as individual personality traits. These include the pressure to publish, the emphasis on secrecy and competition in the research process, and inadequate interaction between young researchers and their mentors. However, the individual still remains ultimately responsible for his or her conduct. Urges the National Institutes of Health to establish a new office to encourage the responsible conduct of research.

(149)
SCIENTIFIC fraud: hearings, 1989 May 4 and 9
US Congress House Committee on Energy and Commerce, Subcommittee on Oversight and Investigations
US Government Printing Office: Washington, DC, 1989. 334pp (Serial No. 101-64)
This hearing looks in detail at the Baltimore case as well as general issues relating to the regulation of misconduct in the biomedical sciences.

(150)
ALLEGATIONS of dishonesty in research and their treatment by American universities
Mazur, A
Minerva, Summer/Autumn 1989 27(2/3) pp177-94, 19 notes and references
Reviews the responses of universities in the early to mid-1980s, noting the reluctance of many to adopt formal investigatory procedures and the resultant difficulty of judging whether particular cases were handled properly. Looks at a range of cases, including some well known ones, arguing that university responses are frequently inappropriate including attempts at a cover-up, retaliation against whistleblowers, and attempts to divert responsibility for investigation to other institutions with which the accused is involved. Discusses ways in which the response to misconduct can be improved.

(151)
MAINTAINING the integrity of scientific research: hearing, 28 June 1989
US Congress House Committee on Science, Space and Technology, Subcommittee on Investigations and Oversight

US Government Printing Office: Washington, DC, 1990. 1,455pp, bibliography pp1411-55 (Serial No. 73)

A major review covering a wide range of issues relating to the regulation of misconduct in the biomedical sciences. These include scientific accountability, the editorial policies of scientific journals, the education of young scientists, institutional responses to allegations of misconduct, peer review, the role of the legal process, and the role of the federal government. A hearing summary is also available

See also: Maintaining the integrity of scientific research: hearing (summary), 28 June 1989 (US Government Printing Office, Jan 1990. 15pp)

(152)

RESPONSIBILITIES of awardee and applicant institutions for dealing with and reporting possible misconduct in science: final rule

US Public Health Service

Federal Register, 8 Aug 1989 54(151) pp32446-51

The final National Institutes of Health rules on misconduct which deal entirely with the responsibilities of universities, omitting those of the NIH itself. The contrast between these rules and the lack of formalised, public procedures within the NIH was one of the factors leading to the collapse of the Office of Scientific Integrity/Office of Scientific Integrity Review system.

(153)

ARE scientific misconduct and conflicts of interest hazardous to our health?

US Congress House Committee on Government Operations

US Government Printing Office: Washington, DC, 1990. 80pp, bibliography (House Report 101st Congress, 2nd session, No. 101-688)

Covers ten cases of misconduct at five universities: Harvard, Florida, Pittsburgh, California (San Diego) and Yeshiva. Highly critical of university procedures in cases of scientific misconduct, but with substantial dissenting views on matters of fact and policy.

(154)

SCIENTIFIC misconduct: the evolution of method: professional ethics report

Hallum, J and Hadley, S

Newsletter of the AAAS, 1990 (3) pp4-5

A review by the director and his deputy of the first year's working of the Office of Scientific Integrity. Claims successful resolution of over 60 cases using the 'scientific dialogue' approach, and challenges claims that OSI methods give insufficient protection to the accused.

(155)

INSTITUTIONAL responses to cases of fraud and misconduct in science: a media roundtable at the National Press Club, June 22 1989

American Association for the Advancement of Science, 1333 H Street NW, Washington, DC 20005, Jan 1990. 32pp

An edited transcript of discussions between journalists and four scientists involved in the National Conference of Lawyers and Scientists' investigation into fraud and misconduct.

(156)

COMPARISON of research quality guidelines in academic and nonacademic environments

Nobel, J J

Journal of the American Medical Association, 9 Mar 1990 263(10) pp1435-37, 3 references
A survey of medical schools in the USA and Canada shows that only two of 133 responding institutions have policy guidelines in place to address misconduct issues. For more on guidelines in 16 medical schools
See also: Medical school guidelines for investigating misconduct and fraud in science, by Z Annau (Accountability in Research, 1992 2(3) pp179-87, 18 references)

(157)
HONOR in science: 2nd edition revised and enlarged
Sigma Xi, The Scientific Research Society, PO Box 13975, Research Triangle Park, North Carolina 27709, 1991. 41pp, 34 notes and references
Practical advice to those entering careers in research on why honesty is important. Discusses types of misconduct, the nature of research as a cooperative activity, whistleblowing, and where to get help if one witnesses or suspects fraudulent activity. For the proceedings of a Sigma Xi forum on a wide range of ethical and misconduct issues
See also: Ethics, values, and the promise of science: forum proceedings (Sigma Xi, 1993. 255pp)

(158)
MISCONDUCT in science: recurring issues, fresh perspectives: conference executive summary, November 15-16 1991, Cambridge, Massachusetts
American Association for the Advancement of Science, Directorate for Science and Policy Programmes, 1333 H Street NW, Washington, DC 20005, 1991. 19pp
A conference sponsored by the National Conference of Lawyers and Scientists, and the Office of Scientific Integrity Review. The sessions deal with the definitions and boundaries of research misconduct; possible policy approaches to the problem; and the rights, risks and responsibilities of whistleblowers.

(159)
SCIENTIFIC fraud: hearings, 6 Mar, 1 Aug 1991
US Congress House Committee on Energy and Commerce, Subcommittee on Oversight and Investigations
US Government Printing Office: Washington, DC, 1991. 260pp (Serial No. 102-75)
Includes coverage of the Robert Gallo case as well as continuing discussion of general misconduct issues and the response of the National Institutes of Health and individual universities.

(160)
SCIENTIFIC fraud and the Public Health Service Act: a critical analysis
Hansen, K D and Hansen, B C
FASEB Journal, Aug 1991 5(11) pp2512-15
FASEB = Federation of American Societies for Experimental Biology. Reprints s493 of the Act which requires those organisations applying for federal research funding to have in place procedures for investigating and reporting alleged scientific misconduct. It also requires the National Institutes of Health to respond to any information received. Discusses s493 in the context of the NIH *Policies and procedures for dealing with possible misconduct in science* (Ref. 143 above), and the establishment of the Office of Scientific Integrity and Office of Scientific Integrity Review.

(161)

SCIENTIFIC misconduct in academia: a survey and analysis of applicable law
Sise, C B
San Diego Law Review, Apr/May 1991 28(2) pp401-28, 199 references
A detailed analysis of the nature of scientific misconduct, self-regulation by the scientific community, and the applicability of the law. For other studies discussing legal aspects in the American context
See also: Legal medicine: the ombudsman of medical ethics, by B J Ficarra (Journal of Contemporary Health Law and Policy, Spring 1987 (3) pp151-67, 41 notes and references)
More gold and more fleece: improving the legal sanctions against medical research fraud, by J T O'Reilly (Administrative Law Review, Summer 1992 42(3) pp393-422, 137 notes and references)
Criminal liability for misconduct in scientific research, by S M Kuzma (University of Michigan Journal of Law Reform, Winter 1992 25(2) pp357-21, 202 notes and references)
Integrity in science: administrative, civil and criminal law in the USA, by D H Sharphorn (Journal of Exposure Analysis and Environmental Epidemiology, 1993 3(1) pp271-81, 14 notes and references)

(162)

ENGINEERING and the law: scientific misconduct – Part 1: the federal rules
Walter, C and Richards, E P
IEEE Engineering in Medicine and Biology, Dec 1991 10(4) pp69-71
The first in a series of articles discussing federal statutes and regulations on misconduct, their effects on researchers, and ways of managing the risks involved. The Engineering and the Law column in this journal is a regular source of useful information on policy and practice developments relating to scientific misconduct in the USA. For the remaining parts of this particular series of articles
See also: Scientific misconduct – Part 2: what are your constitutional rights, by E P Richards (Mar 1992 11(1) pp73-75)
Scientific misconduct – Part 3: standards for scientific record keeping, by E P Richards and C Walter (Jun 1992 11(2) pp88-90)
Scientific misconduct – Part 4: the costs of hubris, by C Walter and E P Richards (Sep 1992 11(3) pp77-79)
Scientific misconduct – Part 5: making scientific self-regulation work, by C Walter and E P Richards (Dec 1992 11(4) pp102-104)
Scientific misconduct – Part 6: constitutional rights revisited, by C Walter and E P Richards (Mar 1993 12(1) pp130-32,39)

(163)

FRAUD in scientific research: the prosecutor's approach
Willcox, B L
Accountability in Research, 1992 2(2) pp139-51, 46 notes and references
The US Attorney from the US Department of Justice, District of Maryland, who prosecuted in the Stepehen Breuning case, rejects the scientific community's view that the legislative or judicial oversight of science would deter people from entering research. Describes such a view as hogwash. Selective criminal prosecution in the most blatant cases, combined with the 'enlightening effect of Congressional interest' has done more to cast light on the 'incestuous dark corner' of fraud than all the self-policing efforts of the scientific community.

(164)
THE INSTITUTIONAL Review Board: ethical gatekeeper
Cohen, R L and Ciocca, A J
In: Research fraud in the behavioral and biomedical sciences, edited by D J Miller and
      M Hersen
      Wiley: Chichester, 1992 pp204-21, 10 references
A useful summary of the role of the IRB in monitoring the ethical conduct of research
involving human subjects funded by the Department of Health and Human Services. For
relevant articles on the issue of misconduct from its own journal
See also: Fraud and misrepresentation in research: whose responsibility? by H S
Wigodsky (IRB: A Review of Human Subjects Research, Mar/Apr 1984 6(2) pp1-5)
Should IRBs monitor research more strictly? by N A Christakes (IRB: A Review of
Human Subjects Research, Mar/Apr 1988 10(2) pp8-10)
Sharing scientific data 1: new problems for IRBs, by J E Sieber (IRB: A Review of
Human Subjects Research, Nov/Dec 1989 11(6) pp4-7)
Research fraud, misconduct, and the IRB, by S Hilgartner (IRB: A Review of Human
Subjects Research, Jan/Feb 1990 12(1) pp1-4, 25 notes and references)
On being an authentic scientist, by M L Smith (IRB: A Review of Human Subjects
Research, Mar/Apr 1992 14(2) pp1-4, 12 references)

(165)
RESPONSIBLE science: ensuring the integrity of the research process:
Volume 1
Panel on Scientific Responsibility and the Conduct of Research
National Academy Press: Washington, DC, 1992. 199pp, bibliography
A wide ranging report covering issues such as scientific principles and research practice;
the contemporary research environment; the incidence and significance of misconduct;
institutional experience of handling misconduct; and guidelines on responsible research
practices. For comment on the National Science Foundation's critical response
See also: NSF fuming over Academy's misconduct report (Science and Government
Report, 15 May 1992 12(9)pp5-6)

(166)
RESPONSIBLE science: ensuring the integrity of the research process:
Volume 2
Panel on Scientific Responsibility and the Conduct of Research
National Academy Press: Washington, 1993. 275pp
Includes background papers covering the role of universities and professional societies in
encouraging responsible research conduct; mentorship and research training; the federal
regulation of research; Congressional activities in relation to scientific misconduct and
integrity; and published guidelines from a variety of universities and national
organisations

(167)
GOOD science and responsible scientists: meeting the challenge of fraud and
misconduct in science
Teich, A H and Frankel, M S
American Association for the Advancement of Science, Directorate for Science and
Policy Programs, 1333 H Street NW, Washington, DC 20005, Mar 1992. 35pp, short
bibliography
A follow up to the three project reports published in 1988 and 1989, and the subsequent

media roundtable (Refs. 144, 155). Focuses on helping research institutions respond to the misconduct problem, arguing that its modern history begins with the William Summerlin affair in 1974. Reviews developments in the issue since then, including the response of scientific journals, scientific associations and research institutions.

(168)
THE OFFICE of Scientific Integrity
Hamilton, D P
Kennedy Institute of Ethics Journal, Jun 1992 2(2) pp171-75, 2 references
Presents a brief description of the origins of the OSI, its approaches and procedures, and legal and other challenges which it faced. Suggests that if the OSI fails it will mean that scientific dialogue has failed as a means of resolving misconduct issues. As a result the scientific community may be forced to relinquish its ability and right to manage its own affairs. The story of the legal challenges to OSI, and of calls for reform in its procedures, was closely followed by the newsy science journals in the USA. For some of the more substantial comment
See also: NIH misconduct probes draw legal complaints, by B J Culliton (Science, 20 Jul 1990 249(4966) pp240-42)
Advisory committee urges changes at OSI, by A Gibbons (Science, 29 Nov 1991 254(5036) pp1287-88)
NSF combines scientific, legal expertise in handling misconduct, by P S Zurer (Chemical Engineering News, 3 Feb 1992 70(5) pp17-19)
OSI: better the devil you know, by D P Hamilton (Science, 13 Mar 1992 255(5050) pp1344-47)

(169)
THE UNITED States government scientific misconduct regulations and the handling of issues related to research integrity
Price, A R
Journal of Exposure Analysis and Environmental Epidemiology, 1993 3(1) pp253-64
Outlines the government and Congressional response to the misconduct issue since the early 1980s, including the PHS regulations published in 1989 which defined misconduct and required institutions in receipt of PHS funding to have policies and procedures in place. Also summarises the role of the Office of Research Integrity, describes its procedures, and presents a hypothetical case study of an ORI investigation. For another article in the same issue of this journal
See also: Introduction to misconduct in science and scientific duties, by C L Soskolone (Journal of Exposure Analysis and Environmental Epidemiology, 1993 3(1) pp245-51, 18 references)

(170)
SCIENTIFIC misconduct: new definition, procedures, and office: perhaps a new leaf
Rennie, D and Gunslaus, C K
Journal of the American Medical Association, 17 Feb 1993 269(7) pp915-17, 31 references
Discusses the establishment of the Office of Research Integrity following the collapse of the Office of Scientific Integrity and Office of Scientific Integrity Review. Focuses particularly on the definitional problem and the agonising it has produced, arguing that it would be more effective to identify what constitutes good scientific practice rather than concentrating so heavily on the bad.

(171)

WHISTLEBLOWER protection: agencies' implementation of the whistleblower statute has been mixed

US General Accounting Office, PO Box 6015, Gaithersburg, MD 20884-6015, Mar 1993. 15pp (GAO-GGD-93-66)

Reviews the response of 19 agencies to the implementation of the 1989 Whistleblower Protection Act and other relevant legislation, noting that most do not inform all employees of their rights. For further comment on the continuing pressures under which whistleblowers operate in the USA

See also: Legal protections for the scientific misconduct whistleblower, by P Poon (Journal of Law, Medicine and Ethics, 1995 23(1) pp88-95)

Veteran whistleblowers advise other would-be 'ethical resisters' to carefully weigh personal consequences before taking action (Scientist, 15 May 1995 9(10) pp1,15)

(172)

FRAMEWORK document on managing financial conflicts of interest

Association of American Universities, One Dupont Circle NW, Washington, DC 20036, May 1993. 17pp

Deals with issues associated with increasing academic-industry links and the possible implications for the integrity of the research process.

(173)

SHATTUCK Lecture: misconduct in medical research

Dingell, J D

New England Journal of Medicine, 3 Jun 1993 328(22) pp1610-15, 19 references

John Dingell was chairman of the Subcommittee on Oversight and Investigations of the US House of Representatives, and a key factor behind increasing Congressional pressure on the scientific community to address the misconduct issue. His lecture, delivered to the Massachusetts Medical Society in May 1992, is critical of scientists, the officials of research institutions and the editors of scientific journals. It aroused the ire of many in the scientific community. For editorial comment, letters and a response from the then director of the National Institutes of Health

See also: The frustrations of scientific misconduct, by J P Kassirer (New England Journal of Medicine, 3 Jun 1993 328(22) pp1634-36, 20 references)

Shattuck Lecture: misconduct in medical research (letters), by D Baltimore and others (New England Journal of Medicine, 2 Sep 1993 329(10) pp732-34, 13 references)

The Dingell hearings on scientific misconduct: blunt instruments indeed, by B Healy (New England Journal of Medicine, 2 Sep 1993 329(10) pp725-27)

(174)

MISCONDUCT: views from the trenches

Taubes, G

Science, 27 Aug 1993 261(5125) pp1108-11

More on institutional policies relating to scientific misconduct including comment on those developed by the Harvard Medical School, University of California (San Francisco) and the University of Illinois.

(175)

INTEGRITY versus misconduct: learning the difference between right and wrong

Pritchard, I A

Academic Medicine, Sep 1993 68(9) ppS67-S71, 13 references

Argues that the principles of scientific integrity are a better basis for the education of young scientists in ethical conduct than an approach which focuses specifically on misconduct. The latter approach only identifies prohibited behaviour while the former is a much more positive force for promoting good behaviour. Also includes comment on the inherent limitations of appealing to academic freedom as an excuse for shielding scientific practice from scrutiny. For another article from this issue of *Academic Medicine*, which is devoted to the theme of integrity in biomedical research
See also: Overlooking ethics in the search for objectivity and misconduct in science, by S J Reiser (Academic Medicine, Sep 1993 68(9) ppS84-S89, 8 references)

(176)
SANCTIONS for research misconduct: a legal perspective
Dresser, R
Academic Medicine, Sep 1993 68(9) ppS39-S43, 15 references
Looks at the legal principles which could be employed in the design and administration of a response to scientific misconduct, noting the difficulty of developing fair and consistent approaches in the absence of agreement on the nature and seriousness of misconduct. Three types of legal remedies are identified as influencing the selection of sanctions in past cases: the quasi-contractual legal remedy of restitution; the philosophy of retribution; and the philosophy of deterrence. All have some merit, but the choice between them will crucially affect the research community's perceptions of the fairness and efficacy of the system. For another article in the same issue of *Academic Medicine* which focuses on the need for a spectrum of responses to match the spectrum of offences
See also: Sanctions and remediation for research misconduct: differential diagnosis, treatment, and prevention, by E G Shore (Academic Medicine, Sep 1993 68(9) ppS44-S48, 6 references)

(177)
SHOULD the government assure scientific integrity?
Klein, D F
Academic Medicine, Sep 1993 68(9) ppS56-S59
Questions the values of the rather 'Orwellian' Office of Research Integrity, arguing that its purported social benefits could be achieved more effectively by other means. Recommends an independent, non-profit investigative agency staffed by scientific and legal experts. This would achieve the objective of removing government from regulation of the scientific community, and would relieve universities of the conflicts inherent in investigating and judging the conduct of their own members. For more on the debate on the relative merits of self-policing and government regulation, including practical suggestions on how the research community can improve its own standards and thus obviate the need for government interference
See also: A call for the development of 'Good Research Practices' guidelines, by J L Glick and A E Shamoo (Accountability in Research, 1992 2(4) pp231-35)
The role of federal regulations in assuring research quality, by P J Friedman (Accountability in Research, 1993 3(2/3) pp111-16, 5 references)
Self-policing and reinforcement as alternatives to government regulation for quality assurance in science, by J Allison and others (Accountability in Research, 1993 3(2/3) pp137-45, 21 references)

(178)
RESPONDING to allegations of research misconduct: a practicum
American Association for the Advancement of Science, 1333 H Street NW, Washington, DC 20005, Nov 1993.

A notebook of materials prepared for the 'practicum' organised by the AAAS/American Bar Association National Conference of Lawyers and Scientists in November 1993. The aim is strictly practical: what to do when allegations are made, how to conduct an inquiry, how to keep records, how to deal with the press and federal authorities etc. A second practicum was held in December 1994, and the notebook of materials for this event is also available from the AAAS

See also: Investigating allegations of research misconduct: a practicum (AAAS, Dec 1994)

(179)
TEACHING scientific integrity and the responsible conduct of research
Sachs, G A and Siegler, M
Academic Medicine, Dec 1993 68(12) pp871-75, 10 references
Describes the scientific integrity training programme introduced by the University of Chicago in response to federal guidelines requiring all students supported by National Research Service Award training grants to receive 'instruction about the responsible conduct of research'. For another article in the same issue of *Academic Medicine* which focuses on the course developed for students of biomedicine at Virginia Commonwealth University

See also: Graduate teaching in principles of scientific integrity, by F L Macrina and C L Munro (Academic Medicine, Dec 1993 68(12) pp879-84)

(180)
TEACHING the responsible conduct of research through a case study approach
Association of American Medical Colleges, 2450 North Street NW, Washington, DC 20037, 1994. 218pp
Based on a large number of case studies focusing on the biomedical sciences but relevant to all disciplines. Covers a wide range of unethical behaviour ranging from plagiarism and taking data to misappropriating knowledge gained during participation in peer review.

(181)
THE PATHOLOGY of research fraud: the history and politics of the US experience
LaFollette, M
Journal of Internal Medicine, Feb 1994 235(2) pp126-35, 29 notes and references
A useful summary of developments in the USA since the early 1980s.

(182)
FACULTY policies on integrity in science
Harvard University Faculty of Medicine, 25 Shattuck Street, Boston, Massachusetts 02115, Jul 1994. 21pp
Harvard has been in the forefront of developing institutional guidelines to the problem of misconduct. This compilation includes the following statements published since the early 1980s: guidelines for investigators in clinical research (Oct 1991); guidelines for investigators in scientific research (Feb 1988); principles and procedures for dealing with allegations of faculty misconduct (Jan 1983); Faculty of Medicine statement on research sponsored by industry (Oct 1983); policy on conflicts of interest and commitment (Mar 1990); amendments to policy on conflicts of interest and commitment (Dec 1993); letters of reference (Apr 1982); and guidelines for editors and authors of medical textbooks

(Sep 1993). For further comment on the 1991 Guidelines and their application
See also: Integrity in science: misconduct investigations in a US university, by M L
Dale (Journal of Exposure Analysis and Environmental Epidemiology, 1993 3(1)
pp283-95)

(183)
VALUES and ethics in the graduate education of scientists
Lapidu, J B and Mishkin, B
American Journal of Pharmaceutical Education, Fall 1994 58(3) pp333-38, 19 references
Reprinted from *Ethics in higher education*, edited by W H May (American Council on
Education: Washington, DC, 1990). Looks in general terms at the need for more explicit
ethical guidance, noting that, until recently, fundamental issues such as the
unacceptability of data falsification or plagiarism were rarely mentioned: students are
expected to know that these things are wrong. Looks at how the issues have been
approached by individual universities such as Yale, Harvard and Michigan.

(184)
ANNUAL report: 1994
Office of Research Integrity, Suite 700, 5515 Security Lane, Rockville, MD 20852,
1995. 33pp
The ORI's second annual report. Allegations of fabrication and/or falsification formed
the basis of 24 of the 26 cases concluded in 1994, but only 15% of all requests received
actually resulted in an inquiry. Eleven hearings resulted in a finding of proven
misconduct. The ORI also publishes a bi-monthly *ORI Newsletter.*

(185)
CODE of medical ethics: current opinions with annotations
American Medical Association Council on Ethical and Judicial Affairs
American Medical Association, Order Department, PO Box 7046, Dover, Delaware
19903-7046, 1995. 177pp
The code is accompanied by judicial opinions and other comment on a wide range of
issues relating to ethical behaviour in the delivery of health care and the conduct of
medical research.

(186)
ON being a scientist: 2nd edition
National Academy of Science: Washington, DC, 1995. 27pp
The National Academy's guidance document for young scientists, originally issued in
1989.

(187)
PLAGIARISM suit wins: experts hope it won't set a trend
Taubes, G
Science, 26 May 1995 268(5214) p1125
Brief comment on the case of Pamela Berge who pursued a plagiarism suit using the
False Claims Act, and won substantial damages. The scientific misconduct community
fears that more plaintiffs might be encouraged to use the courts rather than mechanisms
within the scientific world. For further comment on this case and its aftermath
See also: ...As US reviewer resigns over slur, by R Dalton (Nature, 15 Jun 1995
375(6532) p529)

(188)
FINAL rules put universities in charge
Mervis, J
Science, 21 Jul 1995 269(5222) p294
Brief comment on the new rules on conflict of interest imposed on recipients of funding from the National Institutes of Health and the National Science Foundation. These require researchers to inform their institutions if they, their spouses or dependent children have financial interests (exceeding $10,000 or 5% ownership) in companies that might be affected by their research. The institution then has the responsibility for deciding whether there is a conflict of interest, developing measures to resolve it, and informing the government. The development of the rules, which have the status of a federal regulation, was prompted by the Genentech controversy in which several researchers involved in the clinical trials of a genetically engineered anti-clotting agent developed by Genentech were found to have financial ties with the company.

3.2 European countries, Australia and others

Even the most cursory glance at the literature of scientific deception reveals a glaring discrepancy between the United States and the rest of the world. Although the American scientific community has demonstrated many of the characteristics of scientific conservatism, and has perhaps been forced to confront misconduct by the threat of legislative action, it has shown itself considerably more willing to admit that a problem exists than its counterparts elsewhere in the world. It has discussed the issues exhaustively, developed institutional procedures for investigating and disciplining misconduct, devised guidelines on ethical conduct, and addressed the educational needs of young scientists. Much of this has happened in the public domain, with the newspaper press playing a significant role. Elsewhere there is almost complete silence, with a few isolated exceptions. As the listing below shows there is the occasional general article here, the odd case report there, but nothing to compare with the wealth of literature on the American experience.

France

The position in France, described by Lagarde and Maisonneuve in *Fraud and misconduct in medical research* by Stephen Lock and Frank Wells, may well be typical of many countries (Ref. 197). Although there are some signs that the scientific community is beginning to take the problem of misconduct seriously, the traditional stance of 'it doesn't happen here' combined with resentment of any outside interference still seems to prevail (Ref. 193). The introduction of standard procedures for good clinical practice by American-owned pharmaceutical companies has been 'upsetting to many investigators' and although 'private discussions between investigators, and between personnel of pharmaceutical industries, easily bring up suspicious cases', little seems to have been done in response.

There are, apparently, instances of publication fraud in France but 'owing to the Latin mentality, and to the way French scientific journals are run, these are never disclosed'. Editorial boards often prefer to hush things up rather than publish retractions, and many French journals have insufficient resources to ensure proper peer review. At the institutional level cases remain confidential, with the cover-up the most common form of reaction. Some progress has been made in the area of clinical research fraud with the publication of regulations by the Ministry of Health on good research practice (in line with European Commission guidelines noted below), and the introduction of a medical and pharmaceutical inspection system to monitor laboratories. However, the creation of an institution like the Office of Research Integrity 'is not at all a priority in the scientific community'.

Denmark

In Denmark the response has been much more vigorous although, until relatively recently, Danish scientists tended to believe that the problem was a specifically American one. However, a small group of university teachers with particular responsibility for the ethical training of young researchers became convinced that action was necessary, perhaps before unexpected scandal forced a panic response. Two members of the group were a chairman and former chairman of the Danish Medical Research Council, and the DMRC has been the focus of the response. In 1991 a national commission was set up with a wide-ranging remit to define scientific misconduct and develop procedures for dealing with it. Membership included representatives of the DMRC, university medical faculties, the Danish Medical Society, the Royal Dental Colleges, the Royal Danish School of Pharmacy, the *Journal of the Danish Medical Association*, the central scientific-ethical committee and individual experts.

The commission's report (in Danish and English) was published in 1992 after an extensive analysis of conceptual issues, the lessons offered by particular cases, and the experience of the American scientific community in dealing with the problems (Ref. 192). The climate in which it was received will be familiar to analysts of scientific deception in many countries: support within the scientific community for the fight against dishonesty, combined with a general assumption that informal codes of conduct are quite adequate to deal with the rare cases which occur; a general lack of formalised procedures within universities to deal with misconduct, combined with persecution of whistleblowers and resentment of political interference (described as 'trolls smelling Christian blood'); and a generally low level of public interest in the problem of deception.

The DMRC system is based on the introduction into the scientific community of the principles and practices of democracy and the rule of law including a clear distribution of roles, an agreed conceptual system, quasi-legal procedures including the right of representation, and procedures for appeal. The investigatory framework consists of two regional committees with scientific and legal members nominated by universities, hospitals, government research institutes and, interestingly for a British observer, the Danish Association of County Councils and certain municipal authorities. The national Danish Committee on Scientific Dishonesty (DCSD), which acts as the point of appeal, is staffed from similar sources with the legal chairman required to possess the necessary qualifications for appointment as a High Court judge. A variety of sanctions for misconduct is prescribed ranging from a reprimand from the employing organisation to dismissal or demotion. In between lies transfer to other work or another institution, deprivation and/or repayment of public funding, removal of the right to teach, and the stripping of academic degrees. Equally importantly, the system also allows for the public attestation of the innocence of scientists against whom no case is proved.

The measured and careful nature of the DCSD response is at least partly due to its belief that 'the important aim in dealing with scientific dishonesty is not to unmask the transgressors but to use the lessons learned from the rare and serious cases of scientific fraud to prevent it in future, primarily by teaching good research practice, and its ethical base, during all phases of research education'. In this context Denmark already has the advantage of many other countries in that the requirement for ethical training has been formalised for some years. The DCSD approach, with its emphasis on due process and the importance of addressing some of the factors which produce deceptive behaviour, has much to recommend it as a model for other countries including the UK.

For those interested in monitoring developments in scientific dishonesty across the world, the DCSD annual report of its first year's work is a useful source of information (Ref. 200). Part of its remit is to keep abreast of developments in other countries and to 'profile the Danish investigatory system in the international research community'. As a result, 'DCSD had, from the beginning, a clear interest and priority in gathering literature and information in the field'. Although it has limited resources for sorting and cataloguing material, Appendix 6 of the annual report does list some potentially useful references (for example, on developments in Norway and the Netherlands) which have not been found during the searches for this review. Unfortunately, the bibliographical detail given is often rather limited and, for this reason, they are not reproduced here. However, the DCSD and its secretariat does promise to 'be of assistance in making these materials available'.

Chapter 2 of the DCSD annual report also gives a brief summary of developments elsewhere in Europe, principally in the Nordic countries. In Sweden the Medical Research Council held a conference on misconduct in October 1993, and reached agreement on the need for a Swedish initiative on the Danish model. In 1994 the Finnish National Research Ethics Committee published guidelines on research practice which have been accepted by all universities and major research institutions, and are to be made available in English translation. Norway has also been active, establishing a committee in 1992 to investigate the issue of scientific dishonesty. It took the view that the work done by the Danish could form the basis for decision making in Norway, and that there was no need for a specifically Nowegian study. It prepared a consultative briefing on the issues and will take action once all comments have been received.

European initiatives

The DCSD also notes the establishment of the European Medical Research Councils, a sub-division of the European Science Foundation which considered the problem of scientific dishonesty during 1989-90, concluding that it was a national problem which needed national solutions. Nonetheless, it established a panel on medical ethics in June 1992 which subsequently decided that there was a need for general guidelines for use in member countries with very different research practices and traditions. A recent article in the *Lancet* by David Evered and Philippe Lazar of the EMRC reiterates the need for individual organisations to develop their own guidelines, but stresses the importance of general principles (Ref. 201).

These include clear lines of responsibility for supervising and training young scientists; clear guidance on sound research practice; good record keeping (for at least five years after publication); the provision of advice and training in statistical methods; full evaluation and statistical verification of all data before submission for publication; the restriction of authorship to those 'who have contributed significantly to the work'; the proper citation of relevant work published by others; and the provision of sufficient experimental detail to allow independent evaluation and replication of the research. The EMRC also offers guidelines on reducing the pressure to publish, limiting the impact of financial pressures on researchers, and investigating alleged malpractice.

Evered and Lazar advise research institutions to take account both of the EMRC's general principles, and the guidance produced by other bodies including Harvard University Medical School, the International Committee of Medical Journal Editors and the European Commission's Committee on Proprietary Medicines. The EC's *Good clinical practice for trials of medicinal products in the European Community* is now widely followed by the pharmaceutical industry and has had a significant impact on the development of measures to tackle drug trial misconduct in the UK (Ref. 190). Although directed primarily at the pharmaceutical industry, the GCP guidelines are 'pertinent to all four phases of clinical investigation of medicinal products, including bioavailability and bioequivalence studies, and can be applied more widely by those who undertake experimental investigation in human subjects'. On a broader level, the European Commission has also considered the ethical problems relating to modern biomedical research, and compiled a directory of relevant expertise in this area (Ref. 196).

Australia

Australia has been the source of some of the highest profile cases of scientific misconduct in recent years including the Michael Briggs and William McBride affairs. According to Norman Swan's analysis published in *Fraud and misconduct in medical science*, the Australian scientific community exhibits many of the same unattractive characteristics as its counterparts elsewhere: persecution of whistleblowers, a tendency to take the word of powerful men for granted, and a greater concern for institutional reputations than the integrity of science. The self-correcting mechanisms of science do not prevent fraud, and the scientific community's ability and willingness to police itself properly are in doubt. Perhaps it is only fair to say that Swan is a television journalist who played a major part in bringing the McBride case to public attention (Ref. 195).

The Briggs and McBride cases, and the media attention they attracted, were instrumental in forcing the scientific community to act and, in November 1990, the National Health and Medical Research Council (NH&MRC) introduced new guidelines and procedures which had to be in place by the beginning of 1992 in all institutions applying for funding. The existing condition of award which provided for the termination of a grant 'the research for which is not being carried out with competence, diligence, and scientific honesty and integrity' was apparently ineffective although, to be fair, it could have had no effect in the McBride case which involved activities in an independently funded research institute. Like the Danes, the Australians drew heavily on American experience in developing a system which suits their own particular circumstances.

The NH&MRC statement emphasises the scientific community's responsibility both to itself and the public to maintain 'high ethical standards, and validity in the collection and reporting of data'. Research workers have 'a duty to ensure that their work enhances the good name of their institution and the profession to which they belong'. They should not participate in work which breaches ethical standards and, in cases of doubt, should seek advice from colleagues or peers – 'debate on, and criticism of, research work are essential parts of the research process'.

More detailed guidelines are laid down on data gathering, storage and retention; publication and authorship; the supervision of research trainees; disclosure of potential conflicts of interest; and the procedures to be followed when misconduct is suspected. In the context of what may or may not be defined as misconduct, the statement makes clear that 'honorary authorship is an unacceptable practice' while multiple publication of papers based on similar data is 'improper' unless full cross-referencing occurs. Simultaneous submission of such papers should be disclosed to each journal or publisher involved. As far as potential conflicts of interest are concerned 'the NH&MRC will require disclosure of all affiliations with, or financial involvement in, any organization or entity with a direct commercial interest in any research it supports, from 1991'.

The guidance on misconduct investigation procedures is closely allied with that issued by the Australian Vice Chancellors' Committee and covers the protection of interested parties (including whistleblowers); the receipt of complaints by specially trained senior staff experienced in research and in the literature of scientific deception; preliminary investigations; formal investigations; and action. Due process is stressed and, while 'confidentiality remains important', it should not be allowed to compromise the protection of the accused, the complainant or the public. For example, if charges are dismissed it may well be important for the accused to be publicly exonerated; if they are proven, the complainant may need public recognition to prevent future victimisation. Finally, there may be cases in which journals need to be informed about fraudulent material which may pose a danger to the public. No specific guidance is given on sanctions, merely that 'the institution should take disciplinary action quickly' if a person is found guilty. Relevant publishers and funding agencies should also be informed.

(189)
A QUESTION of fraud: forum
Anderson, I
New Scientist, 28 Apr 1990 126(1714) pp87-88
Deals with the issues in an Australian context, focusing on the guidelines laid down by the Garvan Institute of Medical Research in Sydney. Argues that the vast majority of scientists act according to high ethical standards. For more comment on the incidence of fraud in Australia
See also: How much scientific fraud is there? by B Walby (Interdisciplinary Science Reviews, 1990 15(2) pp108-10, 3 references)

(190)
GOOD clinical practice for trials on medicinal products in the European Community
Committee on Proprietary Medicinal Products Working Party
European Commission: Brussels, 1991. 27pp (111/3976/88-EN Final)
Establishes principles of good clinical practice in respect of trials on medicinal products using human subjects. Although directed primarily at the pharmaceutical industry, they are also of relevance to others involved in the generation of clinical data. They cover the protection of trial subjects and the consultation of ethics committees; the responsibilities of the sponsor, monitor and investigator; data handling issues, including archiving; statistical practices; and quality assurance. This report subsequently led to the following Directive and Corrigendum, which gives statutory effect to the guidelines and has been in force since July 1992
See also: Commission Directive of 19 July 1991 modifying the annex to Council Directive 75/318/EEC on the approximation of the laws of member states relating to analytical, pharmacotoxicological and clinical standards and protocols in respect of the testing of medicinal products (91/507/EEC) (Official Journal of the European Communities, 26 Sep 1991 (L270) pp32-33)

Corrigendum to Commission Directive 91/507/EEC of 19 July 1991 modifying the annex to Council Directive 75/318/EEC on the approximation of laws of member states relating to analytical, pharmacotoxicological and clinical standards and protocols in respect of the testing of medicinal products (Official Journal of the European Communities, 22 Nov 1991 (L320) p35)

(191)
HIMALAYAN fraud rocks Indian science
I Anderson
New Scientist, 9 Feb 1991 129(1755) p17
Comments on the case of Professor V J Gupta who was suspended from his post (and subsequently reinstated) for allegedly falsifying Himalayan fossils. For more discussion
See also: Himalayan palaeontology: Gupta faces suspension, by K S Jayaraman (Nature, 21 Feb 1991 349(6311) p645)
Indian palaeontology: back from the dead, by J Maddox (Nature, 13 Feb 1992 355(6361) p578)
Indian rope trick (Nature, 20 Feb 1992 355(6362) p660)
Gupta's return: pressure grows on Punjab University, by K S Jayaraman (Nature, 12 Mar 1992 356(6365) p97)
Palaeontology under a Himlayan shadow, by J Maddox (Nature, 16 Dec 1993 366(6456) p616)

(192)
SCIENTIFIC dishonesty and good scientific practice
Andersen, D and others
Danish Medical Research Council, H C Andersens Boulevard 40, DK–1553, Copenhagen V, 1992. 126pp, 111 references
Looks in detail at a selection of the more prominent cases of scientific deception; discusses the nature of the scientific process; sets out a system of investigatory committees; makes recommendations on sanctions; and examines measures to promote good scientific practice and prevent dishonesty. For comment on the Danish approach
See also: Scientific dishonesty: the need for precise concepts and effective tools, by P Riis (Journal of Internal Medicine, Mar 1993 233(3) pp213-14, 6 references)
Fraud in medical research: the Danish scene, by P Riis (In: Fraud and misconduct in medical research, edited by S Lock and F Wells. BMJ Publishing: London, 1993 pp116-27, 18 references)
Scientific dishonesty: a Danish proposal for evaluation and prevention, by P Grandjean and D Andersen (Journal of Exposure Analysis and Environmental Epidemiology, 1993 3(1) pp265-70)
Prevention and management of fraud – in theory, by P Riis (Journal of Internal Medicine, Feb 1994 235(2) pp107-16)

(193)
SCIENTIFIC fraud (Les fraudes scientifiques)
Recherches, Feb 1992 23(240) pp254-64 (In French)
Includes three articles, the first on the Baltimore case and the second on the Himalayan fossil scandal involving V J Gupta. The third looks briefly at the response of the French scientific community to the misconduct issue, noting that fraud is very rarely detected. The scientific community is quite certain that existing methods of monitoring and evaluating research make misconduct most unlikely, and is firmly opposed to any action on the American model. For three letters in response to these articles, one expressing

considerable concern at the complacency of the French scientific community
See also: The promising future of scientific fraud (L'avenir prometteur des fraudes scientifiques) (Recherches, Jun 1992 23(244) pp770-71. In French)

(194)
SCIENTIFIC misconduct in medical research
Verma, B L and Shukla, G D
Journal of the Indian Medical Association, Aug 1992 90(8) pp222-25, 17 references
Focuses mainly on scientific misconduct in the developed world but notes that cases are now beginning to appear elsewhere. Includes brief comment on Indian experiences; discusses the factors behind scientific misconduct in medical research; and outlines remedial measures.

(195)
BARON Munchausen at the lab bench?
Swan, N
In: Fraud and misconduct in medical research, edited by S Lock and F Wells
    BMJ Publishing: London, 1993 pp142-57, 16 references
Discusses the background to the development of guidelines by the Australian National Health and Medical Research Council in the wake of the Briggs, McBride and Prasad cases. The NH&MRC statement is reprinted as an appendix (pp187-95). For journal comment by Norman Swan (who is a television journalist), and for a summary and comment on the NH&MRC statement
See also: The exposure of a scientific fraud, by N Swan (New Scientist, 3 Dec 1988 120(1641) pp30-31)
Preventing and dealing with scientific fraud in Australia, by N Swan (Medical Journal of Australia, 1989 150(3) pp169-70, 15 references)
An NH&MRC code for the conduct of science, by I McCloskey (Medical Journal of Australia, 19 Nov 1990 153(10) pp574-75, 8 references)

(196)
DEALING with ethical problems linked to modern biomedical research
Van Steendam, G and others
European Commission Directorate-General XII: Brussels, 1993. 2 parts (EUR 15264/1; 15264/2)
Part 1: *compendium: analytical inventory of problematic situations* aims to find an effective approach to dealing with the ethical dilemmas raised by biomedical research. Part 2: *repertoire; analytical inventory of European expertise and resources* consists of a directory of experts in ethical aspects of biomedical practice and research in all European Union countries, and non-EU Western European countries.

(197)
FRAUD in clinical research from sample preparation to publication: the French scene
Lagarde, D and Maisonneuve, H
In: Fraud and misconduct in medical research, edited by S Lock and F Wells
    BMJ Publishing: London, 1993 pp108-15, 10 references
Describes the approach to scientific fraud in France, with particular reference to the conduct of clinical drug trials. In most respects, the French scientific community shows little interest in the problem of fraud, and the publishing system is not designed to detect, prevent or deal with it.

(198)

University of Otago guidelines for responsible practice in research and procedures for dealing with allegations of misconduct in research

University of Otago, PO Box 56, Dunedin, New Zealand, 1993.

Although New Zealand has been largely free of detected scientific fraud, its universities are aware of the potential problems. The University of Otago's guidelines are an example of recent initiatives, and are closely based on Australian protocols.

(199)

THE MAKING of blue ostriches: further light on a scientific fraud

Dowson, T A

South African Journal of Science, Aug 1993 89(8) pp360-61, 10 references

Brief comment on a celebrated historical fraud. In 1905 a 'copy' of a southern African rock painting depicting a hunter disguised as an ostrich was published by G R Stow but is widely believed to be a forgery, not least because the original rock painting has never been located. Discusses in some detail how the forgery might have been created.

(200)

THE DANISH Committee on Scientific Dishonesty: annual report '93

Danish Research Councils, c/o Danish Medical Research Council, H C Andersens Boulevard 40, DK-1553, Copenhagen V, 1994. 93pp

The first annual report of the DCSD, which began work in November 1992, notes that none of the allegations of scientific dishonesty brought before it in its first year were substantiated, a fact which speaks well for Danish research. However, clearing researchers of baseless accusations is as important a role as any in the response to scientific misconduct. Describes the information and education activities of the Committee, and summarises the 15 cases it considered during the first year.

(201)

MISCONDUCT in medical research

Evered, D and Lazar, P

Lancet, 6 May 1995 345(8958) pp1161-62, 3 references

Discusses the initiative of the European Medical Research Councils in drawing up general guidelines on scientific misconduct to inform research institutions in member countries.

3.3 United Kingdom

While the specific approaches adopted by the USA, Denmark or Australia may not be directly applicable to British circumstances, the experience of all these countries (and others) is of relevance in a world in which science is rightly seen as an international activity. Scientists certainly seem to exhibit very similar attitudes about misconduct regardless of their nationality or location. It is, therefore, hardly surprising that much of the British scientific community can be described as still in a state of denial. However, the *British Medical Journal* and the *Lancet* have campaigned for some time, claiming that there is now sufficient evidence of deception in the biomedical field to warrant the establishment of something akin to the Office of Research Integrity. Stephen Lock, a former editor of the *BMJ,* and now at the Wellcome Foundation, has played a major role, while the editor of the *Lancet* argues that 'for far too often this country has swept cases of fraud under the carpet. It doesn't happen often but, when it does, we need to assure the public that allegations of fraud are investigated properly'.

Research ethics committees

British scientists (especially in the biomedical field) are, of course, not lacking in ethical guidance. The Royal College of Physicians (RCP) and the Medical Research Council have published guidelines on research involving patients, and there are Research Ethics Committees (RECs) in place in health authorities designed to protect the human subjects of medical research. In an interesting parallel with present concerns over scientific misconduct, the establishment of these committees (and their US equivalent, the institutional review boards) was also achieved in the teeth of opposition from elements in the scientific community despite mounting evidence that unethical experiments were being performed on humans and animals. Henry Beecher in the USA and Maurice Pappworth in the UK both had to resort to public exposure of distasteful and dangerous practices before the first Helsinki Declaration on human experimentation could be passed (Ref. 202)

However, an analysis of the role of RECs by the King's Fund Institute suggests that they are not always an adequate check on unethical conduct, a finding which seems to mirror experience elsewhere in the world (Ref. 211). In theory their work is governed by a series of stringent guidelines produced by the Royal College of Physicians (RCP) and the Department of Health, both of which require RECs to assess the scientific validity of research proposals and consider possible conflicts of interest (a particularly important issue given the fact that RECs are overwhelmingly concerned with pharmaceutical trials) (Refs. 206, 207).

In practice many RECs lack the skills to assess the scientific validity of proposals, and a major recommendation of the King's Fund Institute report is the establishment of separate research committees to work alongside RECs to vet research for quality and the likelihood of its achieving its stated objectives. Nor, despite the exhortations of the RCP and the government, do all RECs examine issues of monetary inducements to doctors, researchers, research subjects or other people involved in research projects. 'All the chairmen said that they rely heavily on the goodwill and honesty of colleagues or doctors' and, where unethical conduct is detected, sanctions are often limited. For example, it is a disciplinary offence in some health authorities to conduct research on human subjects without consent, but not in all.

Royal College of Physicians

Increasing British interest in the issue of scientific misconduct has focused on the RCP and the Association of the British Pharmaceutical Industry (ABPI). In January 1989 the RCP set up a working party to consider the issues in response to Stephen Lock's *BMJ* editorial of the previous month (Ref. 61, Ch. 2) and its report, published in February 1991, draws heavily on the experience of other countries such as the USA, Australia and Denmark (Ref. 208). Misconduct is described as a long standing problem, and the RCP identifies a range of familiar causal factors of which professional vanity and the pressure to publish are seen as the most influential. Others include the desire for academic advancement, personal financial gain and outright psychiatric illness.

A range of preventive and investigatory measures is discussed but, unlike the requirements imposed on American universities by regulation as a condition of receiving federal research funding, they have only advisory status. They include attention to the ethical education of scientists, the careful supervision of young researchers, the development of proper guidelines on authorship, the retention of raw research data for inspection for a number of years, and the regular review by departmental heads of publication records. There should also be procedures in place for the investigation of allegations and their subsequent referral to the General Medical Council (GMC) if appropriate. Some universities no doubt have such procedures in place but they do not appear to be within the public domain and there is no way of knowing whether they conform to the RCP guidelines.

Association of the British Pharmaceutical Industry

The second guidance document was published by the ABPI for its member companies in May 1992 (Ref. 210). This was prompted by the RCP report and by the ABPI's own guidelines on good clinical research practice originally published in 1988 (Ref. 209). The latter emphasise the importance of monitoring and audit procedures, and subsequent editions are in line with the European Commission's guidelines which have been in operation since July 1992 (Ref. 190). Pharmaceutical companies in Britain can keep up to date with developments in Europe through the regularly updated guide to *Good clinical practice in Europe* produced by PJB Publications (Ref. 218).

The ABPI, like the RCP, claims that 'the conduct of most clinical research is honest and honourable' but that misconduct is an important issue which must be addressed. Practical guidance is given on detection, for example through monitoring patterns and trends in documentation, examining returned clinical trials material and conducting routine, professional statistical examinations of data. All ABPI member companies are required to introduce standard policies and operating procedures for handling suspected misconduct. If detected, fraud should be referred to the GMC for handling by the professional conduct committee, using a standard form of statutory declaration. Consideration may be given to prosecution in the criminal courts but, in most cases, GMC proceedings are preferred as quicker and more effective.

In crude terms, the RCP guidance might be compared with that issued by the Association of American Medical Colleges, while the ABPI approach is akin to that adopted by the US Food and Drug Administration. An analysis of legal and quasi-legal options in the UK by Christopher Hodges in *Fraud and misconduct in medical research* argues that 'suitable procedures are available to cover the proper and fair investigation of suspicions in research sponsored by industry' because of the imposition of appropriate obligations in contracts, and the introduction of standard operating procedures. However, 'greater difficulties might exist in pursuing suspicions in non-industry sponsored research' (Ref. 213).

Indeed the robust nature of the ABPI approach to misconduct contrasts markedly with the agonising over personal sensitivities and freedoms which seems characteristic of the academic environment. The majority of recent successful GMC proceedings on fraud, usually involving General Practitioners, have resulted from pressure exerted by the pharmaceutical industry. Perhaps this is because a breakdown in the relationship between a company and a GP clinical researcher can be viewed simply as a straightforward breach of contract. The delicate ethical and professional issues involved in research which is further removed from the market often do not apply.

Should more be done?

Public awareness of scientific misconduct, and pressure on the political establishment to do something about it, have clearly been important factors in the United States and

Australia. In Britain awareness appears to be at a lower level, although scientific misconduct has occasionally been the subject of television programmes, most recently in the BBC *Horizon* series (Ref. 48, Ch. 1). In recent months the press has reported the alleged falsification of evidence in the case of the world's 'first' AIDS case, David Carr, who died in 1959 – a story which was the lead item in the *Independent* on 24 March 1995 (Ref. 221). There has been widespread coverage of the case of Dr Malcolm Pearce whose downfall was reported both in the press and on television, and there has also been interest in overseas cases which strike a chord with British readers like those involving the National Surgical Adjuvant Breast and Bowel Project (Refs. 217, 223-225).

One might view these press reports as an interesting and potentially explosive combination of two public (and, therefore, media) obsessions. On the one hand is the pervasive interest in all things medical; on the other, is the late twentieth century concern with sleaze, misconduct and the apparently widespread decline in moral standards among groups which have traditionally been respected by ordinary people. The public is increasingly aware of the financial and ethical pressures under which medicine labours and, while this is often translated into support for doctors, there is also a sense in which the exposure of uncomfortable realities has destroyed the pedestal on which they used to stand. Although there is little direct evidence to suggest that the public is becoming more cynical about medical practice and research, many ordinary people are no longer in the mood to take the moral integrity of professionals for granted.

Moreover, their views, however ill-informed and partial they may sometimes be, carry increasing weight at a time when the traditional system of Parliamentary democracy is under pressure as never before. Public opinion can be both volatile and suspicious of authority, and can exercise considerable influence over the actions of politicians who face an insecure future. In a situation such as this the biomedical research community, while continuing to emphasise the high standards of ethical conduct of most of its members, might conclude that a free and frank admission of occasional problems is a prudent strategy. A continued insistence that misconduct 'doesn't happen here' could rebound disastrously if more cases are revealed.

Implications of government science policies

To date British political interest in the subject of scientific misconduct has been noticeable by its absence – there is no equivalent of John Dingell in the Houses of Parliament. However, one might argue that this is an area which deserves much greater attention from policy makers if only because of the coincidence between government science policy objectives and some of the factors which analysts see as contributing to the propensity for deception. The over-arching theme, affecting all parts of the public sector, is the government's attempt to restrain public expenditure which, in the academic context, has led to a growing mismatch between the amount of research which might be done and the funds available. Competition for research funding from all sources is intense and it is not unreasonable to assume that some in the scientific community will resort to unethical tactics in order to secure or increase their share.

Government might argue with some justification that it cannot be held responsible for unethical responses to funding restrictions which are unavoidable. However, there are aspects of the public management of science with a much more direct influence on the climate for deception including the introduction of quantitative measures of research performance, based in part on publication counts. The impact of such measures on the pressure to publish cannot be denied and, while multiple publication or salami slicing may not rank very high on the deception ladder in moral terms, they are damaging to science because they muddy the waters. According to a recent article in *Research Fortnight*, they also promote behaviour which is more characteristic of the football club's quest for league success than the pursuit of research excellence. Particularly reprehensible is the poaching of individual researchers or research teams with a proven track record in attracting funding (Ref. 220).

The government's decision to introduce performance assessment based on 'objective' indicators of various kinds is, of course, understandable. However strapped for cash the universities feel themselves to be, they are spending very large amounts of taxpayers' money, and it is right that they should be publicly accountable. Unfortunately, the introduction of such measures and their direct linking to the survival of departments inevitably encourages universities to play the system, with the danger that ratings become more important in research planning and management than the research itself. Moreover, there seems to be little place for an ethical dimension in this hard-nosed vision of research excellence. Unlike their American counterparts, British universities are not required to establish misconduct policies or ethical training programmes as a condition of receiving public funding.

Although the 1996 research assessment exercise has dropped the use of total publication counts in favour of the four best papers published by an individual in the previous three years, the universities are already allegedly deep into their own version of fantasy football. Meanwhile, all the major publishing houses are under pressure to publish research studies before the next research assessment deadline in March 1996. Indeed, a Lampeter-based company, Edward Mellen Press, is offering academics a special service – 'meet university deadlines through our 90 day refereed book publishing program' – at a cost of £595. Normal academic publishing, for example by Cambridge University Press, is free to the author but takes around a year after a protracted refereeing process which can last up to six months. Desperate academics may well feel that the cost is justified since the research assessment exercise takes no account of the publisher when submitted work is evaluated (Ref. 226).

The wealth creation imperative

A second strand of government science policy which may be influential in the context of deception is the explicit harnessing of the nation's scientific effort to wealth creation objectives through initiatives like the Technology Foresight Programme (Ref. 222). Universities are encouraged to develop closer relationships with private industry or other non-governmental bodies (research charities, for example), and praised if they increase the proportion of their research income derived from these sources. Again, there are strong arguments in favour of closer academic-industry links in the interests of wealth creation, but potential disadvantages which policy makers need to recognise.

One, which has already been noted earlier, is the massive increase in short-term contract working among young scientists fuelled both by closer academic-industry links and the funding constraints on the universities (Refs. 133, 134, Ch. 2). The pressures on ethical principles imposed by job insecurity and poor levels of reward may well be difficult to withstand whether they relate to personal temptation or the observed misconduct of others. Other potential problems include the biasing of the research effort towards the commercial objectives of specific companies, the commercial appropriation of publicly funded research results, and pressure on academic researchers to deliver positive results at a time determined by commercial rather than research criteria. Conflicts of interest are a very real possibility in the university of the 1990s, and are one of the issues to be examined by the Nolan Committee on standards in public life when it turns its attention to the academic sector later in 1995.

The Pearce case

The response to the Pearce case makes clear that some elements in the biomedical research community are only too aware of the dangers posed by scientific deception and are determined to take quick and decisive action in the absence of a lead from other authorities (Refs. 223-225). Dr Malcolm Pearce's report of the successful transfer of a five-week-old embryo from a patient's Fallopian tube to her uterus was published in the *British Journal of Obstetrics and Gynaecology* in August 1994, and was shortly followed by a internal inquiry at St George's Hospital in South London when colleagues claimed to know nothing about the operation. As a result Pearce was dismissed from his post as a senior consultant in December 1994, and a GMC disciplinary hearing followed in June 1995.

Although Pearce claimed at one stage of the inquiry to be suffering from manic depression – a classic tactic of the scientific deceiver at bay – the GMC found him guilty on twelve charges of serious professional misconduct after a three day hearing. It removed him from the medical register with immediate effect, pending any appeal, and castigated him not only for damaging science but threatening public safety and confidence in research. He 'personally sought to mislead others, implicating others, including junior doctors, in a web of deceit' and his actions had 'incalculable consequences for public confidence in the integrity of research'.

They have also proved a distinct embarrassment to the scientific journals – including the *British Medical Journal* and the *Lancet* – which published Pearce's work. An investigation by St George's Hospital Medical School into 23 papers written or co-written by Pearce is underway but the two papers published in the August 1994 issue of the *British Journal of Obstetrics and Gynaecology* have already been exposed as fraudulent. Not only was Pearce an editor of this journal, his departmental head (Professor Geoffrey Chamberlain) was both editor-in-chief and president of the Royal College of Obstetricians and Gynaeocologists. Professor Chamberlain, who was an honorary co-author of one of the papers, has subsequently resigned from both posts although it was he who ordered the initial investigation of Pearce's claims.

Stephen Lock's comment that 'the time has come for Britain to abandon its lax approach to scientific fraud' and the 'amateurism' that allows fraudulent research to be published seems only too justified (Ref. 227). Professor Chamberlain has admitted that 'I rubber stamped this paper out of politeness and because he asked me to as head of the department'. He, and other Pearce co-authors, have received letters from the GMC reminding them of their responsibilities to check research before allowing their names to be appended to articles but this is unlikely to be enough, on its own, to prevent the publication of fraudulent research. Professor Chamberlain also points out that 'the paper was peer reviewed twice, both medically and statistically. It never occurred to the referees that the whole thing might be a lie'. This despite the apparent crudity of a fraud which claimed that Pearce had seen 191 women at St George's over a three year period with a condition so uncommon that a major referral centre would not expect to see more than one or two new cases a month.

Future developments

Immediately following the conclusion of the Pearce case, the RCP approved a policy resolution to bring together interested parties to discuss the establishment of a central body to coordinate investigations into misconduct. Representatives from the academic science community, the pharmaceutical industry, general practice and the law will be invited to participate along with the Royal Society, despite its recent rejection of the fraud problem as 'miniscule'. A consultative paper will be issued and is likely to recommend a body to receive complaints, commission investigations and, possibly, carry them out itself in certain circumstances, It could also have an educative role in promoting good research practice, and may act in an advisory capacity to those who witness or suspect fraudulent behaviour.

Much of what the RCP and Stephen Lock are proposing builds on the experience of overseas countries such as Denmark and the USA, but it is by no means certain that quasi-judicial approaches of this kind will gain universal approval. John Maddox in a *Nature* editorial published in May 1994 argued that the American model is ineffective both in its own context and as a blueprint for the UK. Efforts to improve accountability should be directed at the institutional level, principally through the imposition of 'administrative fines' on those whose approach to misconduct is judged to be inadequate (Ref. 216). In June 1995, in the wake of the Pearce affair, this strategy was reiterated in another brief editorial which argues that 'reaction in Britain to the serious case of scientific misconduct at St George's Hospital is getting out of hand'. A central monitoring body would be 'toothless' unless established by statute, and 'only people's employers are in a position to impose sanctions on transgressors'.

This is not entirely true, especially in the medical research field. Presumably any central body established as a result of the RCP initiative would have close links with the GMC, and fraudulent researchers would face the ultimate sanction of removal from the medical register. However, in the context of non-medical research, Maddox does have a point. A central body, while it may exert considerable informal influence simply by publicising misconduct issues, will have no powers of its own to impose sanctions such as dismissal or exclusion from public research funding. These matters rest with employing organisations and the funding bodies, and it is widely recognised that many of the former are reluctant to face up to their responsibilities in this area. However, quite who would administer the Maddox system of fines or develop monitoring procedures and standards is not clear.

Perhaps this should be a role for the research councils and the Higher Education Funding Councils and, in the context of biomedical and some social sciences research, the major charities funding work in the universities. Whether or not a system of fines is appropriate or practical, there could well be a case for these bodies taking action to develop a common position on the ethical conduct of research, developing appropriate published guidelines for universities, and (crucially) linking their adoption to the award of funding. At the very least they should ensure that the RCP and ABPI guidelines are widely publicised within the academic community.

There are already some signs of movement, with the Medical Research Council 'planning a clear sanctions package, coupled with rigid procedures for inquiring into scientific fraud designed to safeguard whistleblowers'. It is also drafting a comprehensive document on good research practice. (Ref. 225). In one important area, the archiving of research data as a condition of receiving research council money, the Economic and

Social Research Council already has considerable experience which could be of value to the medical and other research councils. However, as far as the charities are concerned, the Charity Commissioners have rejected proposals to hold medical charities directly responsible for checking on the scientific quality of research published by recipients of their grants. Instead, they are advised to put their trust in journal peer review on the grounds that 'if the results are formally published in a reputable scientific or medical journal, trustees may rely on an evaluation of quality by the journal concerned'. Given the widely publicised inadequacies of peer review, demonstrated most recently by the Pearce case, this recommendation might be described as rather ill-judged (Ref. 230).

On a more positive note, the research councils and other bodies such as the Committee of Vice-Chancellors and Principals, the Royal Society and the various professional associations might also address the need for improved ethical training of researchers to complement the efforts already being made to ensure that, for example, medical students are adequately instructed in the ethics of practice (Ref. 219). The UK Universities Staff Development Unit published a report in 1994 on *Staff development in relation to research* which does begin to address the issues, both in relation to young postgraduate researchers and more senior members of academic staff (Ref. 215). The experience of both the USA and Denmark could also be of value to UK universities in developing policies and training programmes on ethical matters.

Whistleblowing

In a further development of relevance to the scientific misconduct issue, Labour MP Tony Wright has recently introduced a Private Member's Bill to provide whistleblowers with safeguards against victimisation, and compensation for any stress or loss of earnings (Ref. 228). The problems faced by whistleblowers in the NHS have long been a cause for concern, but there have been many other cases in both the public and private sectors (Ref. 214). The charity Public Concern at Work, chaired by the former Director-General of Fair Trading, Sir Gordon Borrie, was set up in 1993 specifically to advise employees and employers on whistleblowing issues and is supporting Mr Wright's Bill which is based on the American model.

In the medical field action has already been taken. In early August 1995 the Secretary of State for Health, Stephen Dorrell, introduced a new duty upon doctors to report on incompetence in their colleagues (Ref. 229). This follows a working party review, chaired by the Chief Medical Officer, and set up in response to a string of notorious cases of misdiagnosis or mistreatment which colleagues ignored. The GMC has already found a consultant anaesthetist guilty of serious professional misconduct for failing to report a colleague's dangerous practices, and it seems likely that the medical establishment will accept the new rule, however distasteful it may be. Some NHS trusts are also inserting clauses into contracts of employment requiring doctors to report to management any incompetence among their colleagues (although, at the same time, routinely including draconian gagging clauses against whistleblowing to the outside world).

While none of these developments are specifically directed against scientific misconduct, they are indicative of a growing concern in the UK about standards of ethical conduct and the pressures imposed on those who seek to expose it. If nothing else, they should give the potential deceiver pause for thought. In the medical field, for example, it is difficult to see how a contractual duty to report practical incompetence could not also encompass a duty to blow the whistle on cheating and corruption in clinical research.

The days are rapidly disappearing when the doctor, the scientist, the lawyer, the teacher, the policeman – indeed any of the elites traditionally accustomed to the unthinking support of the public – could say when faced with criticism 'Trust us – we are professionals'. Too much has happened for that to be any longer a credible response.

The key policy challenge is to re-establish trust and this requires a careful balance between vigiliant monitoring (and, where necessary, disciplining) of behaviour and positive measures to promote good conduct. An over-zealous approach may threaten the very system it is designed to protect – in the words of a recent *Lancet* editorial, 'vigilance amounts to the enforcement of scepticism and distrust; it damages science because trusting is essential to the making of knowledge' (Ref. 227). While it is essential that the scientific community recognises the existence of deceptive behaviour publicly and responds vigorously to it, it is equally (perhaps more) important for it to take measures to revive the 'culture of virtue' on which the historic reputation of science rests.

(202)
HUMAN guinea pigs: experimentation on man
Pappworth, M H
Penguin: Harmondsworth, 1969. 320pp
Pappworth's exposure of unethical practices in research involving human subjects was instrumental in the development of the first Helsinki Declaration on human experimentation, and the establishment of research ethics committees. For his equally influential American equivalent
See also: Experimentation in man, by H K Beecher (Thomas: Springfield, IL, 1959. 230pp)

(203)
THE SOCIAL responsibilities of scientists
Royal Society, 6 Carlton House Terrace, London SW1Y 5AG, 1980. 50pp
The proceedings of a joint meeting of the Royal Society and the American Philosophical Society in June 1980.

(204)
BIAS and fraud in medical research: a review
Pollock, A V and Evans, M
Journal of the Royal Society of Medicine, Nov 1985 78(11) pp937-40, 13 references
A brief review which looks at the avoidance of bias; plagiarism; data falsification; fraud in clinical trials; and the responsibilities of journal editors and referees. Based mainly on American cases and experience

(205)
AN INVESTIGATIVE journalist looks at medical ethics
Campbell, D
British Medical Journal, 29 Apr 1989 298(6681) pp1171-72
Criticises the medical and research councils, and the General Medical Council, for lack of vigour in investigating the activities of Drs James Sharp and Jabar Sultan who conducted a series of highly publicised, but unethical and potentially harmful, experiments with private patients. These came to the public's attention through a television programme. Questions why senior doctors and journal reviewers failed to speak out or alert the General Medical Council, and why the GMC failed to investigate independently. Calls for a national regulatory body to oversee medical conduct in the private sector.

(206)
RESEARCH involving patients
Royal College of Physicians of London, 11 St Andrews Place, London NW1 4LE,
Jan 1990. 53pp
RCP guidelines, together with the advice from the Department of Health listed below,
inform the work of local research ethics committees. For further information
See also: Guidelines on the practice of ethics committees in medical research involving
human subjects: 2nd edition (Royal College of Physicians of London, Jan 1990. 51pp)

(207)
LOCAL research ethics committees
NHS Management Executive
Department of Health: London, 1991. (Health Service Guidelines HSG(91)5)

(208)
**FRAUD and misconduct in medical research: causes, investigation and
prevention**
Royal College of Physicians of London, 11 St Andrews Place, London NW1 4LE,
Feb 1991. 18pp (Also published in Journal of the Royal College of Physicians of
London, Apr 1991 25(2) pp89-94)
The report of a working party set up in January 1989. Identifies types of misconduct, the
factors which may cause it, and measures which can be taken to prevent and deal with it.
For comment by a member of the working party, emphasising the delicacy and
sensitivity of the misconduct issue within the academic environment, and for editorial
comment from the *British Medical Journal*
See also: A head of department's view, by I E Gillespie (In: Fraud and misconduct in
medical research, edited by S Lock and F Wells. BMJ Publishing: London, 1993
pp173-82)
Preventing fraud: the Royal College of Physicians takes its first faltering step, by J Smith
(British Medical Journal, 16 Feb 1991 302(6773) pp362-63, 8 references)

(209)
GOOD clinical research practice guidelines
Association of the British Pharmaceutical Industry, 12 Whitehall, London SW1A 2DY,
1992. Laminated card
These GC(R)P guidelines have been accepted by virtually all UK pharmaceutical
companies and members of the Association of Clinical Research Contractors, and are in
line with the European Commission guidelines listed at Ref. 190. In addition to this
'simple' guide the APBI has produced a range of further guidelines on aspects of clinical
research, most in the form of laminated cards. The final two listed below, which are in
preparation, may be of particular relevance to the non-industrial scientific community.
See also: Medical experiments in non-patient human volunteers (1988, amended 1990)
Facilities for non-patient volunteer studies (May 1989)
Guidelines for ethical approval of human pharmacology studies carried out by
pharmaceutical companies (1990)
Guidelines for Phase IV clinical trials (1993)
Guidelines for the conduct of investigator site audits (1993)
Relationships between the medical profession and the pharmaceutical industry (1993)
Guidelines for company-sponsored safety assessment of marketed medicines (1994)
Clinical trial compensation guidelines (no date)
Good clinical trial practice: guidelines for those engaged in non-industry sponsored trials

(In preparation: designed for academia)
Guidelines on the structure of a formal agreement to conduct sponsored clinical research
(In preparation)

(210)
FRAUD and malpractice in the context of clinical research
Association of the British Pharmaceutical Industry, 12 Whitehall, London SW1A 2DY, May 1992. 14pp + annex
Describes the development of guidelines in other countries, and gives practical advice to member companies. Includes a standard operating procedure for the handling of suspected misconduct, and a standard form of statutory declaration of cases to the General Medical Council. For further comment on the ABPI approach to the misconduct problem
See also: The British pharmaceutical industry's response, by F Wells (In: Fraud and misconduct in medical research, edited by S Lock and F Wells. BMJ Publishing: London, 1993 pp75-90, 9 references)
Fraud and drug research, by D Brahams (Lancet, 22 Aug 1992 340(8817) pp477-78)
Fraud and misconduct in clinical research: is it prejudicial to patient safety? by F Wells (Adverse Drug Reaction and Toxicological Review, 1992 11(4) pp241-55, 13 references)

(211)
ETHICS and health care: the role of research ethics committees in the United Kingdom
Neuberger, J
King's Fund Institute, 126 Albert Street, London NW1 7NF, 1993. 48pp (Research Report 13)
A detailed analysis based on a survey of Research Ethics Committees which are public watchdogs working within the health service to protect the rights of human subjects of medical research. Finds major deficiencies in the operation of RECs, despite the existence of stringent guidelines from the Royal College of Physicians and the Department of Health, and makes recommendations for improvements. For more on this subject, including an analysis by Australian, John Pearn which covers experience elsewhere in the world
See also: Local research ethics committees: report of the 2nd national conference, by J Moran (Journal of the Royal College of Physicians of London, Oct 1992 26(4) pp423-31)
Manual for research ethics committees: 3rd edition, compiled by C Foster (King's College London, Centre of Medical Law and Ethics, Dec 1994. 626pp)
Publication: an ethical imperative, by J Pearn (British Medical Journal, 20 May 1995 310(6990) pp1313-15, 30 references)

(212)
FRAUD and misconduct in medical research: causes and control, a United Kingdom view
Hoffenberg, R
in: Ethical issues in research, edited by D Cheney
University Publishing Group: Frederick, MD, 1993 pp93-100, 13 notes and references

(213)

INVESTIGATING, reporting, and pursuing fraud in clinical research: legal aspects and options in England and Wales

Hodges, C

In: Fraud and misconduct in medical research, edited by S Lock and F Wells

BMJ Publishing: London, 1993 pp91-107, 53 notes and references

A detailed analysis of the applicability of English criminal and civil law, and quasi-legal professional misconduct proceedings, to scientific misconduct in the medical field. In most cases the disciplinary procedures of the General Medical Council are preferable: they generally take less time (six months, on average, from the start of an investigation to a decision), are much less costly, are less formal in procedural terms, and are conducted by people with the requisite clinical knowledge.

(214)

WHISTLEBLOWING in the health service: accountability, law and professional practice

Hunt, G (editor)

Arnold: London, 1994. 192pp

(215)

STAFF development in relation to research

UK Universities Staff Development Unit, Level Six, University House, Sheffield S10 2TN, Mar 1994. 85pp (Occasional Green Paper 6)

Argues that training in support of the research function is essential if universities are to achieve what will be asked of them in the next decade. Looks at the support of staff and examiners in work with research students; at the training of postgraduates in their teaching role; and the support of more senior staff in the management of their own research.

(216)

WHAT to do about scientific misconduct

Maddox, J

Nature, 26 May 1994 369(6478) pp261-62, 2 references

Reviews this problem in the American context, arguing that judicial or quasi-judicial approaches are ineffective. Institutions should be made accountable for the ethical conduct of their researchers, perhaps through a system of fines on those which fail to monitor research conduct adequately. Attention must also be paid to the fundamental cause of misconduct, pressure to publish. For more on this from John Maddox

See also: Making publication more respectable, by J Maddox (Nature, 2 Jun 1994 364(6479) p353)

How to police fraud (Nature, 22 Jun 1995 375(6533) p616)

(217)

TRIALS on trial

Wuethrich, B

New Scientist, 28 May 1994 142(1927) pp14-15

Discusses the upsurge of interest in fraud in clinical trials in the context of the scandal surrounding the National Surgical Adjuvant Breast and Bowel Project's claims about the relative merits of lumpectomy and mastectomy in the treatment of early breast cancer. Although there is apparently no evidence that women have been inappropriately treated as a result, the scandal provoked considerable alarm in the USA and elsewhere. For more on this case from the North American literature

See also: Breast cancer: how to handle misconduct, by D Rennie (Journal of the American Medical Association, 20 Apr 1994 271(15) pp1205-07)
Setting the record straight in the breast cancer trials, by M Angell and J P Kassirer (New England Journal of Medicine, 19 May 1994 330(20) pp1448-50, 31 references)
Science and scandal: what can be done about scientific misconduct? by A Robinson (Canadian Medical Association Journal, 15 Sep 1994 151(6) pp831-834)

(218)
GOOD clinical practice in Europe: 4th edition
Horace, V
PJB Publications Limited, 18-20 Hill Rise, Richmond Surrey TW1 6UA, Jul 1994. 257pp

(219)
TEACHING medical ethics symposium
Journal of Medical Ethics, Dec 1994 20(4) pp229-50
Four articles dealing with the training of medical students in the ethical aspects of medical practice.

(220)
ACADEMICS subvert the ratings game
Research Fortnight, 1 Mar 1995 pp14-15
Discusses the 'fantasy football' being played by vice-chancellors around the country to ensure that they get the right result in the research assessment exercise.

(221)
WORLD'S first AIDS case was false
Independent, 24 Mar 1995 pp1-3
A detailed account of the controversy surrounding the death of David Carr who, it was claimed in a 1990 article in the *Lancet,* was the world's first confirmed case of AIDS. However, exhaustive analysis of tissue samples taken from Carr's corpse have failed to suppport this view and may indicate deliberate tampering with evidence. For subsequent comment alleging that that the Central Manchester NHS Trust refused permission for one of its scientists involved in the 1990 study to send a letter of retraction to the *Lancet*
See also: Admission of false AIDS case was suppressed by NHS (Independent, 6 Apr 1995 p1)

(222)
NEWS and views
Grayson, L
Science Technology and Innovation, Apr 1995 8(2) pp1-11
Summarises developments in the UK Technology Foresight Programme which is designed to link public sector science more closely to the creation of wealth and improved quality of life, and looks at some of the implications for science. Lists all Foresight documents produced to date by the Office of Science and Technology.

(223)
REPORT of the independent committee of inquiry into the circumstances surrounding the publication of two articles in the British Journal of Obstetrics and Gynaecology in August 1994
Royal College of Obstetricians and Gynaecologists, 27 Sussex Place, Regent's Park, London NW1 4RG, 1995.

(224)
TOP doctor 'spun web of deceit'
Independent, 6 Jun 1995 p8
Reports on the General Medical Council investigation into the conduct of Dr Malcolm
Pearce. For later press comment on the GMC's decision, on the subsequent inquiry into
Pearce's publication record, and the Royal College of Physicians' decision on the
establishment of a central investigatory body
See also: Doctor who lied about operation is struck off (Independent, 8 Jun 1995 p3)
Inquiry into medical research papers (Independent, 16 Jun 1995 p2)
College calls for medical research fraud squad (Times, 19 Jun 1995 p5)

(225)
UK fraud verdict prompts move on ethics
Abdulla, S
Nature, 15 Jun 1995 375(6532) p529
Brief comment on responses to the Pearce affair, including plans by the Medical
Research Council to introduce a sanctions package and guidelines on procedures for
inquiring into scientific misconduct. For further comment on the need for a ban on
honorary authorship
See also: Honorary authorship (Nature, 15 Jun 1995 375(6532) p522)

(226)
FAST-track for rush to publish
Times Higher, 16 Jun 1995 (1180) p2
Brief comment on the plans of Edwin Mellen Press to offer academics a 90 day peer
review and publication service to beat the 1996 research assessment exercise deadline.

(227)
LESSONS from the Pearce affair: handling scientific fraud
S Lock
British Medical Journal, 17 Jun 1995 310(6994) pp1547-48, 17 references
Argues that Pearce case shows that the UK has learned little about the handling of
academic scientific fraud despite the Royal College of Physicians' report in 1991.
Focuses particularly on the role of the *Journal of Obstetrics and Gynaecology*, on honorary
authorship, and on the proven inability of the academic scientific community to police
itself. For the *Lancet* view on the need to re-establish a culture of virtue in science
See also: Shall we nim a horse? (Lancet, 24 Jun 1995 345(8965) pp1585-86)

(228)
WHISTLEBLOWER protection Bill
HMSO, Jul 1995. 12pp (House of Commons Bill 152, Session 1994-95)
A Bill introduced by Labour MP Tony Wright, with support from senior Conservative
and Liberal Democrat MPs, the Freedom of Information Campaign and the charity
Public Concern at Work. Mr Wright's attempt in 1992 to get a Bill on whistleblowing
in the NHS passed failed.

(229)
DOCTORS face duty to report deficient colleagues
Independent, 7 Aug 1995 p2
Brief report on the introduction by the Secretary of State for Health of a duty on doctors
to report incompetent colleagues. For more comment
See also: Spot the incompetent doctor (Independent, 7 Aug 1995 p13)

(230)
MEDICAL research charities 'can rely on peer review'
Dickson,D
Nature, 10 Aug 1995 376(6540) p455
Brief comment on the rejection by the Charity Commissioners of proposals to make research charities directly responsible for checking on the scientific quality of the research they fund. Charities are advised to rely on journal peer review instead. The proposals arose from the controversy surrounding the publication of results in 1990 on the use of alternative cancer treatments at a centre in Bristol. The study, which appeared in the *Lancet*, claimed that survival rates of patients at the centre were much lower than for those treated using more conventional means, findings which had to be withdrawn after it was revealed that they were based on faulty statistical analysis.

INDEXES

I. AUTHORS

2. CORPORATE BODIES

This index includes corporate bodies as the subjects, as well as authors and publishers, of documents.

3. SUBJECTS

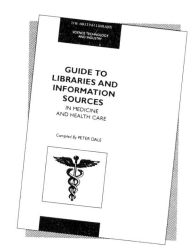